THE CHRISTIAN IN COMPLETE ARMOR

THE CHRISTIAN IN COMPLETE ARMOR

YOUR GUIDE TO CRUSHING THE DEVIL'S LIES
AND WALKING IN SPIRITUAL VICTORY

BILL GIOVANNETTI

ENDURANT PRESS

Copyright © 2023 by Bill Giovannetti

All rights reserved.

No part of this book may be reproduced or transmitted in any form or by any means, digital, electronic or mechanical, including photocopying, recording, or by an information storage and retrieval system—except by a reviewer who may quote brief passages in a review to be printed in a magazine, newspaper, or on the Internet—without permission in writing from the publisher.

Although the author and publisher have made every effort to ensure the accuracy and completeness of information contained in this book, the same assumes no responsibility for errors, inaccuracies, omissions, or any inconsistency herein. Any slights of people, places, or organizations are unintentional. Unless indicated, all hypothetical persons and situations mentioned in this book are fictionalized. The resemblance of any such person to any person, living or dead, is strictly coincidental. Nothing herein shall be construed as a substitute for personal, pastoral, or professional counseling or therapy.

ISBN E-book edition: 978-1-946654-40-3

ISBN Print edition: 978-1-946654-39-7

All Scripture quotations, unless otherwise indicated, are taken from the *New King James Version* (R). Copyright © 1982 by Thomas Nelson, Inc. Used by permission. All rights reserved.

Scripture quotations marked (NLT) are taken from the *Holy Bible, New Living Translation,* copyright © 1996, 2004, 2007 by Tyndale House Foundation. Used by permission of Tyndale House Publishers, Inc., Carol Stream, Illinois 60188. All rights reserved.

Scriptures marked NAS95 taken from the NEW AMERICAN STANDARD BIBLE, Copyright © 1960, 1962, 1963 1968, 1971, 1972, 1973 1975, 1977, 1995 by The Lockman Foundation. All rights reserved. Used by permission. http://www.Lockman.org

For additional resources, please visit maxgrace.com.

DEDICATION

If all the devil's wits and wiles will not serve him to overcome one single soldier in Christ's camp, much less shall he ever ruin the whole army.
~William Gurnall

I have had many wonderful teachers throughout my life, and I am grateful for all of them. It may seem strange, but I would like to dedicate this book to the thousands of authors who have taught me the Word of God, most of whom I have never met. Thank you.

Specifically, I would like to dedicate this book to an author who has literally blessed me from the grave. His name is William Gurnall, and the book for which he is most famous is called *The Christian in Complete Armor*.

This epic treatise on spiritual warfare was first published in three volumes, between 1655 and 1662, in Lavenham, England. It was essentially a compilation of his sermons, as is this present volume. Gurnall, however, was immeasurably more painstaking and detailed than me in his analysis of Paul's great treatise on spiritual warfare in the Epistle to the Ephesians (6:10–17). It amazes me to think that Gurnall's sermons on these eight verses of Holy Scripture can fill over 600 pages of extremely fine print. What kind of pastor can preach such profound and detailed sermons? And what kind of congregation can sit still long enough to hear them? All of this makes me think that today's church—both pulpit and pew—has lost something beautiful and important in our collective appetite for truth. I have replicated Gurnall's title as an homage to him, except for using the American spelling of "armor."

John Newton, that great pastor and the composer of the hymn, *Amazing Grace* said, "If I might read only one book beside the Bible, I would choose *The Christian in Complete Armour*."

Even the Prince of Preachers—and my personal hero—the inimitable Charles Spurgeon said, "Gurnall's work is peerless and priceless; every line is full of wisdom; every sentence is suggestive. The whole book has been preached over scores of times, and is, in our judgement, the best thought-breeder in all our library... This *Complete Armour* is beyond all others a preacher's book: I should think that more discourses have been suggested by it than by any other uninspired volume. I have often resorted to it when my own fire has been burning low, and I have seldom failed to find a glowing coal upon Gurnall's hearth."

So I dedicate this book to William Gurnall, and to every Christian author who has poured heart and soul into words on a page to bless the people of God.

This book before you is one author's humble attempt to follow in the trail others have blazed. After 25 books, I had intended to be finished with writing, but I find I cannot be silent.

There's still a fire in my belly.

The warfare is real. Satan and his hosts are spending their fury, knowing their time is short. We live in dark and perilous times. Our nation is in trouble. Our culture. Our world. Our loved ones. Evil is ascendant. Never has there been a greater need for the everyday women and men of the church to arise. May we stand strong. May we push back the darkness. May we put to flight the hosts of evil.

May the grace of our Lord Jesus Christ be to us an ever-present shield and sword. And may that precious Gospel of Grace flow from our lips to the ears and hearts of a desperately hurting and damned-without-Christ world.

They need *Him*.

So they need *us* to tell of *Him*.

That can only be done as we demolish the devil's strongholds in our hearts, put on our armor, and stand strong and radiant in fulfillment of William Gurnall's—and the Apostle Paul's—grand vision. I pray that each reader of this book will rise up to truly become a Christian in Complete Armor.

For Christ and the Gospel,
Bill Giovannetti

I'd like to offer a huge thank you to Jared Dodson and Garst Peterson for your investment, expertise, and help in making this a better book.

O ye saints, when reproached and persecuted, look farther than man, spend not your wrath upon him. Alas! they are but instruments in the devil's hand. Save your displeasure for Satan, who is thy chief enemy. These may be won to Christ's side, and so become thy friends at last.
~William Gurnall

CONTENTS

Preface	xv
1. ABLE TO STAND	1
Able to Stand	2
Reflection and Discussion	14
2. GOD'S POWER IN THE CHRISTIAN SOLDIER	16
Spirit Beings	16
What Are the Devil and Demons?	17
The Personal Stakes	19
Dominion	20
The Eternal Stakes	22
What Kind of Power Is It?	22
What Will God's Power Do For You?	24
What Does God's Power Feel Like?	26
What Activates God's Power In Our Lives?	28
Reflection and Discussion	31
3. CASTING DOWN STRONGHOLDS	32
Baby Steps	32
Strongholds	34
Casting Down Strongholds	36
Reflection and Discussion	43
4. SIGNS OF A STONGHOLD	45
Demon Possession	45
The Blind Spot	48
Nine Warning Signs of a Stronghold	48
Not Normal	54
Prayer	55
Reflection and Discussion	57
5. WHAT IS THE ARMOR OF GOD?	58
The Windswept House	58
The Dangers of the Unfilled Heart	61
The First Song	66

Prayer	68
Reflection and Discussion	69

6. THE BELT OF TRUTH — 70
   Start Here — 70
   What is Truth? — 71
   Truth is Reality, Therefore… — 72
   Problem — 76
   The Belt — 79
   Reflection and Discussion — 80

7. THE BREASTPLATE OF RIGHTEOUSNESS, PART 1 — 81
   Guard Your Heart — 81
   Your Psyche is Under Attack — 82
   The Breastplate of Righteousness — 89
   Reflection and Discussion — 93

8. THE BREASTPLATE OF RIGHTEOUSNESS, PART 2 — 95
   David and Saul's Armor — 95
   The Breastplate of Righteousness — 97
   I Am the Righteousness of God in Christ — 97
   David and Saul's Armor — 102
   Reflection and Discussion — 106

9. THE BOOTS OF THE GOSPEL — 107
   Wear Your Boots — 107
   Preparation — 109
   The Gospel — 113
   Peace — 119
   Reflection and Discussion — 122

10. THE SHIELD OF FAITH — 124
   The Fiery Serpents — 124
   The Shield — 126
   The Fiery Darts — 127
   The Anatomy of Faith — 129
   The Shield of Faith — 135
   Reflection and Discussion — 138

11. THE FORMULA OF FAITH — 139
   Forgetting the Obvious — 139
   The Formula of Faith — 143

Where Does Faith Come From?	146
Reflection and Discussion	149
12. THE HELMET OF SALVATION	**150**
Spiritual Problems Require Spiritual Solutions	150
The Helmet of Salvation	151
Six Ways Salvation Safeguards Your Mental Health	153
Hosea and Gomer	166
Mental Health is Your Birthright	170
How Do You Wear Your Helmet?	171
Reflection and Discussion	172
13. THE SWORD OF THE SPIRIT, PART 1	**174**
A Hundred Tall Men	174
The Sword of the Spirit	176
Reflection and Discussion	186
14. THE SWORD OF THE SPIRIT, PART 2	**188**
Dominion	188
Back to Babylon	195
Say It…	198
Reflection and Discussion	199
15. THE PROFILE OF A CHAMPION	**200**
The Main Thing	200
The Profile of a Champion	201
Eight Qualities	202
Reflection and Discussion	213
16. ONE THOUGHT TO RULE THEM ALL	**214**
Something Deep	214
One Thought To Rule Them All	216
The One Thought	222
Captivated	226
Reflection and Discussion	228
Epilogue	230
Also by Bill Giovannetti	231

PREFACE

"We are the Borg. You will be assimilated. Resistance is futile."

There is hardly a better analogy to the forces arrayed against traditional values of God and country, family and faith than *Star Trek's* Borg. Irrational mandates, universal corruption, sexually deviant crusaders, anti-God media, arts, and entertainment, the deconstruction of truth, and the relentless pursuit of a New World Order.... all flowing from a "hive mind" that can only represent a world-spirit drunk on the "doctrines of demons" (1 Timothy 4:1).

Mainstream media messaging today comes across more as a sinisterly alluring "Borg Manifesto" than as entertainment or information.

I have a conspiracy theory. I can say it in one word: Satan.

His henchmen are coming for our children, for our traditions, and for our faith. "We are the secular progressives. You will be assimilated. Resistance is futile."

Spoiler alert: in a thrilling two-part *Star Trek Voyager* finale, the Borg—the swarming locust-like scourge of the universe—was exterminated. Resistance wasn't futile and assimilation wasn't inevitable.

Welcome to The Resistance. We are Christians in Complete Armor. By grace through faith, David is still slaying his Goliaths. You are invited to join us.

CHAPTER 1
ABLE TO STAND

In heaven we shall appear, not in armour, but in robes of glory. But here our arms are to be worn night and day. We must walk, work, sleep in them, or else we are not true soldiers of Christ.
~William Gurnall

Finally, my brothers and sisters, be strong in the Lord and in the power of His might. Put on the whole armor of God, that you may be able to stand against the wiles of the devil. For we do not wrestle against flesh and blood, but against principalities, against powers, against the rulers of the darkness of this age, against spiritual hosts of wickedness in the heavenly places. (Ephesians 6:10-12)

WHEN BELIEVERS in Jesus seek to actually experience their blessings from God, we quickly make a startling discovery. There is a host of evil powers clawing at us to keep us far away from the joys and blessings of God.

We are living every moment in the atmosphere of an invisible and fierce spiritual warfare. There is an unceasing war between

God and the devil, heaven and hell, angels and demons, truth and deception.

God loves you and has a wonderful plan for your life, even as the devil hates you and has a devastating plan for your life.

The devil's plan does not confine itself to religion. He's not just fighting to wreck your faith. Instead, he attacks you, tooth and nail, in your emotional health too. Add to that your love life and your sense of confidence.

Even more, he pummels your identity, ambushes your relationships, assaults your friendships, and claws at your morality. He fights your fulfillment, aggresses your gratitude, and harpoons your happiness. If he can, he'll poison your personality, sabotage your sexuality, and contaminate your money. You are in a war, and your enemy considers every aspect of your life the battlefield.

You should do the same.

Satan spews his acid spit onto absolutely everything you touch, and he doesn't play fair. You need to become a Christian in *complete* armor, and that is the purpose of this book. The devil hates the fact that you picked up this book. He will do everything he can to make you put it down.

You've been warned.

ABLE TO STAND

This title comes from the Apostle Paul's epic revelation in Ephesians 6:11, where he commands, "Put on the whole armor of God."

The Greek word, *panoplia,* combines the word *all* with the word *armor* —the full armor of God.

By the end of this book, my goal is that you will know how to put on that armor, and that you will know why God gave you each piece of armor.

Let me illustrate from an episode in the history of God's people, the Jews.

God spoke to their leader, Joshua:

> Moses My servant is dead. Now therefore, arise, go over this Jordan River, you and all this people, to the land which I am giving to them—the children of Israel. Every place that the sole of your foot will tread upon I have given you, as I said to Moses.... Be strong and of good courage, for to this people you shall divide as an inheritance the land which I swore to their fathers to give them. (Joshua 1:2,3,6)

The land is the land of Canaan, and of all people, the Jews have the most ancient claim. Five hundred years before Joshua came to its border—the Jordan River—Abraham already possessed this land. God gave it to them. "Every place the soul of your foot will tread upon I have given you," he said.

The land was theirs. Their name was on it. They had title and deed. It had belonged to them for centuries.

It is the Promised land, a place of blessing, and fulfillment, and purpose, and joy. But here's the big problem: They *owned* the land, but they did not *possess* the land.

So God encourages Joshua. *Let's go! It's time to cross the Jordan River and finally possess your possessions.*

When the Bible talks about spiritual warfare, when we are warned against Satan and hosts of demons, when we are told about a fierce and unceasing conflict, and about doctrines of demons, and deceiving spirits, and the devil transforming himself as an angel of light, when we read of workers of iniquity, and of the Antichrist, and of all of that dark and wicked domain, none of this is meant to scare us.

You should not be afraid. Rather, you should "be strong and of good courage."

Why?

1. Your victory has already been won in Jesus Christ.

Twenty centuries ago, a man named Jesus walked this earth. He taught with astonishing authority. He loved us, he sacrificed his life, and he made claims unlike any other spiritual teacher in history.

In his death, he went nose to nose with the monster called Sin—the plague that has captivated our race since the beginning.

In his resurrection, he not only conquered Sin, he also defeated death, the grave, Hell, Satan, and evil, and he unwound all their consequences.

It's as if Jesus went to a prison, found the human race held captive, vaporized the guards, shattered the prison bars, and set the captives free.

Jesus Christ is the great liberator—not by violence or force and strength alone, but by death and resurrection. He did all this at great cost to himself. And he did this because he loves you.

Think for a moment about Resurrection weekend.

On Friday, Jesus met his death. The Blood of Christ flowed freely down the old, rugged cross. Disciples laid him in a tomb. Soldiers rolled a stone in front of it. Priests sealed it shut.

On that gloomiest of days…

The whole cosmos quaked.

Darkness celebrated.

Demons cackled in glee.

Sin triumphed.

Hell opened wide.

Death reigned supreme.

Satan did his victory dance.

The Great Liberator Jesus was seen as captive, and with his death, all hope of unfettered human potential was lost.

But that was Friday, and Sunday was coming.

There, in the ground, his body lay all night Friday. All day Saturday. The cosmos was holding its breath. Then Sunday came.

Early on that Sunday morning, something happened. Something remarkable. Something unparalleled. Something the devil never saw coming.

The ground started shaking,
the guards started trembling,
the seal started splitting
the demons started screeching,
the devil started raging,
Christ's body started waking,
And when heaven's clock counted down to zero…

> *Up from the grave, he arose!*
> *With a mighty triumph o'er his foes.*
> *He arose a victor from the dark domain*
> *And he lives forever with his saints to reign.*
> *He arose!*
> *He arose!*
> *Hallelujah, Christ arose!*

In that moment:
He conquered death.
He shattered the gates of Hell.
He broke the chains of sin.
He unleashed a flood of forgiveness.
He crushed the devil's head.
He sealed the demons' doom.
He shattered the powers of darkness.
He demolished evil at its source.
And he opened eternal salvation for all who will only believe.
Oh, Victory in Jesus, My Savior forever!
The war is over. The victory is won.

When you think of spiritual warfare, you need to start here. Yes, there's a battle. Yes, there's a fierce and brutal conflict raging all around. But Jesus Christ has won the war. In that sense, the war is over.

But we still need to be Christians in complete armor.
Why?
Because our whole life is part of a mopping up operation. The outcome is certain, but the battle still rages.

2. Therefore, as a Christian, you don't fight *for* victory, but *from* from victory.

This is because the blood of Christ is stronger than the acid spit of Satan, and his blood wipes away every stain.
Do you see what this means?
It means that the victory in every realm is already yours. Your name is on it. You have title and deed. The battle was fought. The victory was bought. It was paid for and it belongs to you. God gave it to you.
Let's get specific. The victory is already won for you in...

- Your emotional health
- Your love life
- Your sense of confidence
- Your identity
- Your friendships
- Your moral virtues
- Your purpose
- Your career
- Your marriage
- Your family
- Your mission
- Your happiness.

True fulfillment is your birthright. A heart of gratitude is your inheritance. A life of abundance is your heritage.
Throughout this book, I'm not urging you to fight and scrap and labor for blessings that aren't yours by rights.

I'm urging you to seize your birthright!

I'm telling you to put on your armor, get it dirty, muddied, and spiritually bloodied. Don't just leave it in the closet. Because that armor holds the key to your abundant life.

I'm telling you to acquire the knowledge and to muster the faith to possess your possessions in Christ.

These gifts of grace are *already* yours.

The wonderful God-blessed life is already yours.

The armor of God is already yours.

The invincible power and unconquerable might of God is already yours.

Your name is already written on mountains and mountains of blessings.

It's time you let your mind believe that, in Christ, you are rich in blessings, and rich in everything that money can't buy.

God gave you the Promised Land before you ever set foot in it. Go get it!

Putting on the armor of God is not how you *win* the victory. Putting on the armor is how you *lay hold of* Christ's victory. It's how you make it your own.

Putting on the armor is nothing other than boldly declaring your faith in the presence, power, plan, and the sufficiency of God. It is declaring to the world and to angels and to demons and to the devil and to God—and even saying to yourself—*God is on his throne, and he loves me, and even though I feel at my worst, I still believe God is at his best, and therefore, no matter how fierce the battle and difficult the way, God has made me "able to stand!" I believe. I take possession of my Promised Land.*

But there is an obstacle to this actually happening. Just like the Jews in Joshua's day. God told Joshua:

> "Pass through the camp and command the people, saying, 'Prepare provisions for yourselves, for within three days you will cross over

this Jordan, to go in to possess the land which the LORD your God is giving you to possess.'" (Joshua 1:11)

The Jews had to cross the boundary of the Jordan River. The *experience* of their victory was waiting for them on the other side.

But for forty years, they refused to cross that river. For forty years, God's own people wandered in the wilderness. They missed out on the Promised Land. They missed out on their victory.

So their testimony was swamped by constant trouble.

- Constant frustration
- Chronic boredom
- Continual attacks
- A lot of needless drama
- A relentless spirit of complaint

The wilderness is not a nice place.

Oh, they were saved. They had been freed from slavery in Egypt. They had crossed through the Red Sea. They were a redeemed people, just like us.

But they stopped short of the Promised Land. They got to the very border of it and their faith faltered. They saw giants in the land. They saw fortified cities in the land. So they quit.

They had left slavery and arrived at the Jordan River in less than one year, but they got scared, turned around, and then wandered in the wilderness for forty years.

You might be re-enacting that story right now. But you can change this. By grace, you can write a new ending.

They could not step into their victory, only because they would not. They would not experience their birthright. They refused, they hardened their hearts, and told God to take a hike. That whole generation went down as casualties in the spiritual warfare of the cosmos.

3. Even though the victory is already yours, your *experience* of that victory stands waiting on the other side of a spiritual barrier.

That barrier is called a "stronghold" and it is inspired by the devil.

People are searching for peace. People are searching for inner wholeness and grace. You need to know that God is standing right where you feel stuck, and he's saying, *Don't quit. Take hold of what is yours. Don't get knocked down or knocked out.*

But you've got to get past this *thing,* whatever it may be. You've got to cross your Jordan. "Prepare provisions for yourself." You've wandered long enough. It's time for you right now to break through the barrier. It's different for everybody.

What's *your* Jordan River? Where do you routinely get stuck?

- Anger
- Despair, hopelessness, or giving up
- Bitterness
- Temptations you can't get past
- A rough childhood
- A painful story of rejection and loss
- Spiritual immaturity
- Loneliness
- Ingratitude
- Apathy
- Addiction or dysfunction
- Stubbornness
- Resentment
- Entitlement
- Self-pity
- You're just tired of it all
- Weary from the fight

Your Jordan River might be chronic doubts about God.

But if you supply the faith, and if you keep moving forward with determination and Holy Spirit Grit, then the God who parted both the Red Sea and the Jordan River will also make a way for you.

He promised. Victory is one hundred percent guaranteed to the person who keeps faith in Jesus Christ.

> "Put on the whole armor of God, that you may be able to stand against the wiles of the devil." (Ephesians 6:11)

It would be a very simple thing if the Adversary of our souls came to us and plainly said, "Hello. I'm going to eat you for lunch. I want to get you into a situation that will cause you a lot of misery, a rapidly fading happiness, a boatload of regrets, and the dishonoring of your Savior. If you will only listen to me, you can stay in this barren spiritual wilderness for your whole pathetic life."

If only the devil were that clear, we could push him back much more easily, but he does not come that way. He is transformed into an Angel of Light (2 Corinthians 11:14), and he is a Master Liar (John 8:44). In fact, the very first lesson in all of Scripture about him is that he is *subtle* (Genesis 3:1).

4. We don't just stand against the devil, but against the "wiles" of the devil.

This word *wiles* means cunning, deceit, trickery. It means to cast a spell so strong and to weave a web of lies so convincing that even the sincerest Christian can be taken in.

Paul asked some very strong Christians, "O foolish Galatians, who has bewitched you?" (Galatians 3:1).

Bewitched. Let that sink in.

Let me mash Joshua back in right here.

God told Joshua to cross over the Jordan where he would find the Promised Land. He would also find seven cursed nations of

Canaan, interlopers. They were corrupt. They were violent and cruel. They were given to all kinds of perversion and idol worship. They were demonized cultures. They were to be destroyed.

But one day a strange looking group of men came limping into Joshua's camp dressed in rags. They were sun-scorched and worn. They had ragged sandals on their feet. In their packs, they carried loaves of bread which had grown moldy and dry along the way. Their goat-skin water bottles were cracked, and their lips were parched.

When the Jewish scouts met them, these men said, "We have come from a very far country. Our sandals were new when we set out. Our bread was fresh. Our water bottles were full and new. We have come such a long way because we have heard of you and how God is with you. Our rulers want to make an alliance with you."

So they said to God's people, "Let's be friends."

> "Then the men of Israel took some of their [moldy] provisions [to investigate]; *but they did not ask counsel of the LORD.* So Joshua made peace with them, and made a covenant with them to let them live; and the rulers of the congregation swore to them." (Joshua 9:14-15, emphasis added)

In biblical terms, a covenant between nations is essentially a formal agreement or treaty that establishes a relationship and sets terms for interaction. This type of covenant is not unlike modern treaties or agreements between nations, but it carries a sacred weight because it is made before God.

Joshua ratified this covenant without reference to God. Do you think that might be a big mistake?

Three days later, Joshua discovered it was all fake. The moldy bread, fake. The worn out sandals, fake. The cracked water bottles, fake. These men had come from a nearby tribe, one of the seven nations under God's curse. Now, they had seduced God's own people into an unholy alliance. A destructive, ungodly covenant—

one that could not legitimately be broken. This bad decision would be a thorn in their side for centuries.

You see, we don't just have to stand against the devil, but against *the wiles* of the devil.

If you're going to prevail, if you're going to be a Christian in Complete Armor, you need to wake up and stay awake. You need to have your alarm system activated.

The devil has worked this scheming, deceptive, dishonest way all throughout the eons of history. He's still doing his dirty tricks today. He's doing them in our culture. In our country. In our world. In society. In social media. In government, arts, entertainment, education. In your school. In your life. In your children.

He makes his offers look so good in so many ways, but every single time there's a very sharp hook in it. There is nothing the devil will offer you that doesn't look good, feel right, or seem like a better option than what God says. When a people or a nation or a child of God does not "ask counsel of the Lord," they fall into the trap set by Satan.

> Finally, my brothers and sisters, be strong in the Lord and in the power of His might. Put on the whole armor of God, that you may be able to stand against the wiles of the devil. For we do not wrestle against flesh and blood, but against principalities, against powers, against the rulers of the darkness of this age, against spiritual hosts of wickedness in the heavenly places. (Ephesians 6:10-12)

5. If you will put on the armor of God, you *will* be able to stand.

No question about it.

If you put on the armor of God, you won't get taken in by the wiles of the devil. You won't take the bait. You won't be shaken, knocked down, or knocked out.

You will stand. You will stand strong and mighty, a loyal warrior in the army of grace and truth.

But you say, It's just too hard. I am not able to stand. That little voice in your head says, I'm too weak. But God says, My strength is made perfect in weakness.

The little voice says, Even if I try, I'll fail. But God says, If I declare you are able to stand, then you are able to stand.

The little voice says, You'll never get across that Jordan. But God says, "When you pass through the waters, I will be with you; And through the rivers, they shall not overflow you" (Isaiah 43:2).

The little voice says, There are giants in the land. But God says, There's a bigger giant here, and I'm on your side.

The little voice says, But God has let me down. But God says, Look at my son, bleeding on that Cross, and then look at that empty grave, then look, if you can, upward, and find a gaze that penetrates into the heavenly realm, and see if you can see Jesus, sitting there, representing you, and making intercession for you, and making a mansion for you, and being your mediator, and your surety, and your ever-present help, and your friend, and your guardian, and your guide, and your deliverer, and your advocate, and your provider, and your victory, and your all-sufficiency, and your sacrifice, and your Savior, and your Supporter, and your soon and coming King... "Oh," God says, "look at HIM and tell me again how I've let you down."

The little voice says, I am undependable. But God says, I am dependable.

The voice says, I am unfaithful. But God says, I am faithful enough for us both. And if you follow me, you will be able to stand.

The little voice in your head says, Life is hard. But God says, These are momentary and light afflictions.

The little voice says, Life is really hard. But God says, There is more to this life than just this world.

The little voice says, Life is really, *really* hard. But God says, It will be worth it all when you see Jesus. Until then, you will be able to stand.

The voice says, I don't have it in me. But God says, I have it in me, and I'll put it in you, so that you will be able to stand.

Never underestimate what God will keep on doing in you when you keep on believing. You *putting on* the armor is how God *puts in* the experience of your blessings in Christ.

If you put on the armor, God will put in the strength.
If you put on the armor, God will put in the joy.
If you put on the armor, God will put in the purpose.
If you put on the armor, God will put in the love.
If you put on the armor, God will put in the peace.
If you put on the armor, God will put in the power.
If you put on the armor, God will put in the contentment.
If you put on the armor, God will put in the character.
If you put on the armor, God will put in the provision.
If you put on the armor, God will put in the wisdom.
If you put on the armor, God will put in the God-blessed life.
If you put on the armor, God will put in the reward.
If you put on the armor, God will put in the victory.

If you put on the armor, God will make the demons flee, and the devil weep, and the angels cheer, the way straight, the rewards more glorious, and your eternity more grand.

Oh put on the Lord Jesus Christ, and you will find yourself in him, and you, the real you, will be ABLE TO STAND.

Welcome to Spiritual Bootcamp.

Let's go!

REFLECTION AND DISCUSSION

1. What are 1 or 2 reasons for why you're reading this book?

2. How real is spiritual warfare to you? How conscious of it are you in your day to day life?
3. Do you believe in the devil? In demons? Why or why not?
4. "Your victory has already been won in Jesus Christ." "You don't fight for victory, but from victory." What are your thoughts and feelings about these statements?
5. What does 2 Corinthians 4:4 say about spiritual warfare and the wiles of the devil? (In each of these sections I will ask you to actually open your Bible, digital or print, and interact with Scripture for yourself.)

CHAPTER 2
GOD'S POWER IN THE CHRISTIAN SOLDIER

If thou dost not stumble at this stone, the devil hath another at hand to throw in the way. He is not so unskillful a fowler as to go with one single shot into the field; and therefore expect him, as soon as he hath discharged one, and missed thee, to let fly at thee with a second.
~William Gurnall

SPIRIT BEINGS

> For we do not wrestle against flesh and blood, but against principalities, against powers, against the rulers of the darkness of this age, against spiritual hosts of wickedness in the heavenly places. (Ephesians 6:12)

There is a vast realm of darkness, and in that realm there are evil spirits, fallen angels. These are called demons, and they march in ranks under their commander, the devil. They are not symbolic. They are not metaphors for or literary personifications of evil. The devil is a literal being with a personality and a name. So are the demons.

Their ranks are listed here in Ephesians chapter six. These and others are mentioned throughout Scripture.

- Demons in the Bible are named 55 times.
- Unclean spirits are named 22 times.
- Familiar spirits, 16 times.
- Spirits, referring to demons, 15 times.
- Evil spirits, 14 times.
- Principalities and powers, 12 times.
- A lying spirit, 4 times.
- A foul spirit, 2 times.
- A jealous spirit, 2 times.
- A spirit of divination, spirit of infirmity, and spirit of error, the angels who sinned, the devil's angels, 1 time each.

WHAT ARE THE DEVIL AND DEMONS?

Scripture is clear that in the original creation, God made a race of intelligent and mighty beings called angels. While their number is not given to us, Scripture does reveal there are myriads and myriads of them.

The highest of these angels was a beautiful creature, named Lucifer. The prophets of the Old Testament reveal both his beauty and his pride. Of his beauty, Ezekiel declares, "You were the seal of perfection, Full of wisdom and perfect in beauty" (Ezekiel 28:14). Of his pride, Isaiah reveals that Lucifer actually said it was his intention to become "like the Most High God" (Isaiah 14:14). This, of course is impossible; it is the pinnacle of hubris.

So at some unspecified time in the misty dawn of cosmic history, Lucifer attempted a coup against the Triune God. He seduced about a third of the angels to come with him (Revelation

12:4). This coup went nowhere. God is omnipotent; Lucifer is not. God is infinite; Lucifer is finite. Lucifer and these angels were cast out of heaven. Lucifer's name was changed to Satan. The angels who fell became demons.

Isaiah's lament is the classic Scripture passage on this horrible fall.

> "How you are fallen from heaven, O Lucifer, son of the morning! How you are cut down to the ground, You who weakened the nations! For you have said in your heart: 'I will ascend into heaven, I will exalt my throne above the stars of God; I will also sit on the mount of the congregation On the farthest sides of the north; I will ascend above the heights of the clouds, I will be like the Most High.' Yet you shall be brought down to Sheol, To the lowest depths of the Pit." (Isaiah 14:12-15)

Jesus said, "I saw Satan fall like lightning from heaven" (Luke 10:18). Peter reveals, "…God did not spare the angels who sinned…" (2 Peter 2:4). John says, in the Book of Revelation, "So the great dragon was cast out, that serpent of old, called the Devil and Satan, who deceives the whole world; he was cast to the earth, and his angels were cast out with him" (Revelation 12:9).

Simply put, Satan and demons are fallen angels.

Some people think that demons are the spirits of dead people. This is absolutely contrary to biblical teaching. There are some people who say that angels are the spirits of people we love who are coming back to visit us. As sentimental and touching as the thought might be, it is also contrary to biblical teaching.

There is also a line of teaching that says demons are some kind of sub-humanoid being created before God created Adam and Eve. Yet another line of teaching identifies demons with the hybrid beings spawned in Genesis 6—suggesting demons are the disembodied spirits of the Nephilim. All of this flies in the face of the clear biblical teaching that demons are fallen angels.

Never forget there is simply no way to obtain any truth about the spirit realm other than by submitting our minds to the revelation of the Word of God. That Word is quite clear about the origins and nature of demons as fallen angels.

THE PERSONAL STAKES

God has revealed something the human eye cannot see, but the human heart knows all too well: *This fallen world is a morally broken pain machine.* And this is because there is a war going on in the spiritual realm.

SPOILER ALERT: The grace of God, through the armor of God, can deliver God's finest blessings anywhere, anytime, to anyone who believes, even beyond the diabolical walls of the broken pain machine.

The devil can't stop God's blessing.

Even so, there is a ruthlessness, a win-at-all-costs mentality, that galvanizes the side of evil that does not exist in the Christian mind.

Evil plays to win and to destroy the opposition. Christians generally play just not to lose.

As Christians, we should never be malicious and mean. We are not called to any violence whatsoever against any individual or group.

I am advocating, pleading, and writing that you first and foremost embrace the reality that you live in a spiritual world engaged in a spiritual war, and that you embrace the idea that the most cherished things in life are at stake: your children, grandchildren, marriage, relationships, finances, retirement, mission and purpose in life, and on and on. Whether or not Christianity survives in our culture is also at stake.

You are at stake. Your identity. Your selfhood. The devil wants to take away your identity. He wants to define you his way, not God's way.

Satan wants to strip your identity and eat your dignity. This is the battle you are in. The devil wants you to be a number, a nameless cog in his machine. He is scrapping and clawing and spitting and fuming to *dehumanize* the human race. You are a thing, an it, an animal. Nothing sacred. Nothing wonderful. Just a bag of matter and energy in the great collective of darkness. You're a nobody. You have no name.

I write to say that I do have a name. My name is Christian. I do have an identity. I am a human. I am a man, I am a husband, and I am a father, and I have a family, I am a sacred human being, the epitome of divine creation, imbued with the miracle of life, made in the image of God and I possess eternal value no animal comes close to. I will not let this decrepit satanic world system squeeze me into its dehumanizing and depressing mold.

Life is a *spiritual* battle, so we need the power of God. With that awesome divine power, we will be able to stand. "Finally, my brothers and sisters, be strong in the Lord and in the power of His might" (Ephesians 6:10).

DOMINION

However, without God's power, we will lose everything precious and good in this life *and* in the life to come.

In the beginning, God gave every human this fantastic gift called *dominion* (see Genesis 1:26, 28). Dominion is the power and God-given right to take charge of your life.

As God was creating us in his own image, it's as if he sliced off a sliver of his [infinite] sovereignty, and imbued human nature with a [finite] bit of it. This is the genesis of our dominion. This theme of dominion will recur throughout this book; it's that important. It's the essence of your battle.

Dominion means to rule your own passions.

It means to rise above your outbursts.

It means to feel love, joy, and peace.

Dominion means freedom. It means liberty.

Dominion means to cast off all that would shackle you, enslave you, and hold you back.

God gave you the crown and the scepter and declares that you are to "reign in life" (Romans 5:17).

But the devil hates human dominion. He's jealous of it.

He wants to be the Lord Most High. So, just as he stole the crown and the scepter from Adam and Eve, even today he is crafting and plotting and manipulating and scheming and cheating and strategizing and lying and anything else he can do—the devil is breaking a diabolical sweat—to steal your dominion.

That means:

To constrict your freedom.

To vaporize your hope.

To do evil against you and convince the world it's okay.

To steal away your dominion, the devil will trap your heart in the snare of depression, or of addiction, or of dysfunction.

Every time you "lose it," give up on life, or check out you are falling short of your dominion.

The devil will divorce sex from marital love, thus subtracting the sacred from the physical, thus erasing the preciousness of eternal souls, thus reducing sex and intimacy to the level of animals.

He will question obvious realities and make *you* feel like the crazy one.

Satan wants you miserable and messed up. He wants you defeated. God makes you a *victor*, but the devil makes you a *victim*. All of that is Satan's plan for you.

How's he doing?

God gave *you* the keys to the kingdom — you're the one who's been opening and shutting the doors. Who have you been allowing in? What have you been allowing in?

The thief comes to steal, to kill, and to destroy. Christ comes that you may have life and have it more abundantly (John 10:10). Resist the devil and he will flee from you.

You are in a war and your personal dominion is at stake. The personal stakes could not be higher.

But even more urgent than all of that, Heaven and Hell are at stake too.

THE ETERNAL STAKES

The devil is doing all he can to suffocate the gospel because his domain is filled with unbelievers. On whether or not you live a life that adorns the gospel, communicates the gospel, and propagates the gospel hinges the eternal destiny of everyone you know and love.

Will they meet Jesus? Will they embrace him as the Savior?

Will they be saved, and by being saved, embrace the only refuge from the wrath of God?

Is there anyone you care about who has not received Jesus Christ? You are to be to them a living example of the power of grace. If the devil can take that away from you, he can make it harder for people you love to be saved.

So the devil is doing all he can to suppress the gospel. He is blinding minds to the gospel (2 Corinthians 4:4).

But he cannot win.

Because the gospel, the message of Jesus Christ crucified and risen again, is the power of God, and ten million devils can never hold it down, even when it is spoken forth by the humblest, weakest, least qualified child of God.

You need the power of God. I need the power of God. Because everything that is precious for eternity depends on it. Be strong in the Lord and in the power of his might.

WHAT KIND OF POWER IS IT?

All throughout this country there are massive towers with thick power lines forming a grid that brings power to every corner of the land.

Now imagine another set of lines running from heaven to you. Those lines are unbreakable. They are all sufficient. They are always in operation. No blackouts. No brown outs. No outs.

God sends down power. It is the power of his might.

It is always perfect. Always enough and more than enough. Always right on time. It is the same power that created the universe. It is the same power that hung the galaxies in space. It is the same power that broke the back of the grave and raised Jesus from the dead.

It is resurrection power.

It's the kind of power you can't work up on your own.

You can't go to school to learn it.

You can't say magic words to get it.

You can't perform rituals to obtain it.

You can't lobby government to bestow it.

You can't look within to discover it.

Look to heaven and look to the God who made it, and he will give you strength.

It's not your power. Not human power. Not carnal power. Not earthly power at all.

There's a prayer in the Bible: That you would know…

> …the exceeding greatness of His power toward us who believe, according to the working of His mighty power which He worked in Christ when He raised Him from the dead and seated Him at His right hand in the heavenly places, far above all principality and power and might and dominion, and every name that is named, not only in this age but also in that which is to come. (Ephesians 1:19-21)

That's the power coming down the lines to you. The same power that smacked the devil's dark domain upside the head can be known and experienced by you.

It is God's power.

It is God's power inside God's soldier.

Because it is God himself inside of you. Christ in you. The Spirit in you. The hope of glory.

Won't you be strong in the Lord and in the power of his might?

WHAT WILL GOD'S POWER DO FOR YOU?

Simply put, God's power will do for you whatever you need whenever you need it.

It is the power to do the right thing when the wrong thing can make your life better, you think.

It is the power to say the kind word when the harsh word is what comes naturally.

It is the power to accept yourself as God accepts you. To see yourself as God sees you. To love yourself as God loves you.

It is the power to be kind to your spouse, gentle with your children, and respectful of your parents.

To be a good dad, a good mom, a good kid, a good employee, and a faithful friend, boyfriend or girlfriend.

The power to work on your marriage. Work on your dating. Work on your relationships.

God's power is there for you.

It's the power to heal your wounds.

To make an alcoholic sober, an addict clean, and a legalist a humble, grace-filled miracle.

It's the power to stay cool under pressure.

To be grateful when life is hard, and faithful when faith makes no sense.

It's the power to choose love, to choose joy, and to find peace.

It's the power to be holy. The power to be whole.

It's the power to evangelize, to speak up for Christ, and to share the gospel.

It's the power to do whatever you need wherever you need to do it and whenever it has to happen.

It's the power to be the person who stands tall and regal and isn't knocked down by the Pain Machine.

> And God is able to make all grace abound toward you, that you, always having all sufficiency in all things, may have an abundance for every good work. (2 Corinthians 9:8)

Paul is saying there is...

- No time, no place, no situation, no circumstance
- No problem, no illness, no loss
- No heartbreak, heartache, addiction, or dysfunction
- No bad news, perplexity, confusion, or doubt
- No assignment, duty, calling, homework, or job
- No relationship, conflict, failure, trial, temptation, or trouble
- No chemical imbalance
- No family of origin chaos
- No locational limitation
- No iron wall, bamboo curtain, or glass ceiling
- No regret, no despair, no enemy
- No economic downturn, no international conspiracy, no intergalactic Death Star
- Do demon, no devil, no demonic attack, no diabolical oppression, no satanic ruse, no devilish abuse
- No wiles of the devil...

But that God has already sent down the line all the power you need to rise above, to thrive, and be more than a conqueror in Christ Jesus.

You have the power to be whole. You have the power to stand. Not just in good times but in bad times too.

That's your testimony.

That's your invincibility.

It's what makes you a loyal warrior in the angelic conflict.

But you might say, If God is sending me power, I sure don't see it. I sure don't feel it. What's that about?

WHAT DOES GOD'S POWER FEEL LIKE?

Here's a truth about God's power that most Christians don't quite understand.

God's power feels like whatever you're feeling when you receive it, because there is no official feeling of the power of God.

When God's power flows, you might feel invincible. Unconquerable. Unbeatable. You might see the answers to your prayers just the way you prayed them. You can see the victory. You can smell it.

In these times, you can almost hear the devil run away.

So when Scripture says you are in a battle and exhorts you to be strong in the Lord and in the power of his might, and to put on all the armor of God, sometimes that power God sends down will feel amazing.

But most of the time, it doesn't.

Listen to this testimony of one of the greatest heroes of the church.

> And lest I should be exalted above measure by the abundance of the revelations, a thorn in the flesh was given to me, a messenger of Satan to buffet me, lest I be exalted above measure. Concerning this

thing I pleaded with the Lord three times that it might depart from me. (2 Corinthians 12:7-8)

Here is this great man Paul, with what he calls his "thorn in the flesh." Nobody knows exactly what that is. Commentators have speculated through the years. Some say bad eyesight. Some say he was hunched over. Some view this as a church person who persecuted Paul. I sometimes suspect this was an actual person who made it his mission to harass Paul. We can't be sure.

I'm glad the thorn in the flesh is not clarified, because it can therefore apply to all of us.

He calls it a "messenger of Satan."

Let's just say thorn in the flesh represents any trouble in your life that needs God's power, God's blessing, and God's intervention.

So he did exactly what he's supposed to do with such a trouble.

He prayed. And he prayed hard.

He pleaded with the Lord. He begged the Lord. Three times he held intense prayer sessions about it. He wanted it to depart from him. "Lord, make it go away!"

But God didn't answer even Paul's prayer the way he prayed it.

By the way, if you don't get answers to prayers the way you prayed them, you're in really good company. This is not a glitch in the system. You didn't do anything wrong.

When God answered Paul's prayer, it wasn't the answer he wanted, but it was the answer he needed.

> And He said to me, "My grace is sufficient for you, for My strength is made perfect in weakness." Therefore most gladly I will rather boast in my infirmities, that the power of Christ may rest upon me. Therefore I take pleasure in infirmities, in reproaches, in needs, in persecutions, in distresses, for Christ's sake. For when I am weak, then I am strong. (2 Corinthians 12:9-10)

This is the great paradox of Christianity, and one of the great lessons about God's power that so few Christians understand.

When I am weak, then I am strong.
When I am tired, then I am strong.
When I am sad, then I am strong.
When I am upset, then I am strong.
When I am afraid, then I am strong

What does the power of God feel like? Like anything. Like nothing. Like everything. It doesn't always feel like power. It doesn't always feel like joy. That's why you can't go by feelings.

You have to go by faith.

WHAT ACTIVATES GOD'S POWER IN OUR LIVES?

Here is a profound secret. Let it sink into your soul.

Victory isn't the victory in our lives as Christians, faith is the victory.

If you activate faith, God activates power. This happens no matter what you feel or don't feel.

Anyone can have faith when everything's going great, but it's faith when faith makes no sense that makes the devil afraid.

Have faith. Keep faith with God. You might feel the weakest, poorest, tiredest, biggest failure as a Christian the world has ever seen.

But when *you* are weak, then *you* are strong, if only you will just keep faith with God.

John declares, "And this is the victory that has overcome the world—our faith" (1 John 5:4).

Victory isn't the victory. Faith is the victory.

The things Christians celebrate and the things God celebrates are different.

We celebrate the win. We celebrate the healing. We celebrate the perfect score and the notable achievement and the fame and the glory and the praise. We celebrate success. We make celebrities of winners.

Heaven celebrates these things too.

But heaven also celebrates someone else.

Heaven will make celebrities out of the woman or man who stayed faithful—who kept believing, trusting, praying, giving, serving, and loving—even when their world caved in.

There's the faith and there's the victory. There's the trembling of the demons. There's the smile of heaven. There's the angels' applause.

There's the greatest miracle of all: a flesh and blood mortal clinging to the naked promise of God when all the evidence and every other voice screams that you're a loser who will never make it.

The devil can't handle you when you do that. You scare him.

When you've prayed 100 times for something to come true, it is prayer 101 that makes heaven applaud, the demons screech, and the devil retreat.

That you would have unanswered prayer after unanswered prayer and yet pray again, just because you believe in a God who loves you--that is a victory of the highest order.

Even if earth never knows your name—and there's no win, no healing, no perfect score, and notable achievement, no fame, no glory, no praise, no social media fame, and no success—as a person who keeps the faith, who is true to your *self* in Christ, and true to God's Word, even if you labor for a lifetime with struggles and questions and doubts… if you keep faith with God, and pray, and believe, and trust… then

IN HEAVEN YOU ARE A CELEBRITY. One day, the angels will line up at the pearly gates to get your autograph.

Because, in the spiritual realm, victory isn't the victory, faith is the victory.

Faith is not the prelude to victory; faith *is* the victory.

God sees your struggles and knows your fears. He honors

forever the faith you have in spite of them. This is God's power inside God's soldier.

God sees the money you saved and then lost and then saved again, and the faith you have to still be generous and brave and kind. God rewards that faith. The devil fears that faith.

God sees your mind, wrestling over his inscrutable ways, but still opening your Bible and seeking to hear his voice there, in the one place where he still speaks.

God sees your love of truth and of the people who need it.

God sees your slim wallet and the residue of your dysfunction. He sees your physical weaknesses and your rejections. He sees the trembling faith that keeps you blundering forward anyway.

God sees your struggle with self-esteem, why it seemed stupid for you to ever think you could conquer addictions, or loneliness, or fear—you said—and sees the true you struggling to break free.

He honors that faith. Stay with him till your victory breaks through. Because God loves faith way more than you've ever dreamed.

Which means that whatever the *earthly* outcomes of your faith may be, in heaven, God has a multiplier. Even the slenderest strand of faith is working for you a far more exceeding and eternal weight of glory.

> For our light affliction, which is but for a moment, is working for us a far more exceeding and eternal weight of glory." (2 Corinthians 4:17)

I know you want to collect your inheritance on earth, but some of it is just going to have to wait till heaven, and on that day it will blow you away.

Let's all just be okay with that.

That doesn't mean to give up on our blessings now. Keep on asking, keep on seeking, keep on knocking on heaven's door.

But if you want to kick the devil in the teeth and have a testimony for Christ and stand strong in the unceasing conflict of the angels, there is no magic incantation, formula, ritual, or school for that.

It's just faith.

It is the power of the Spirit of God plus the Word of God that puts muscle on your faith, and faith is the victory.

So, "Be strong in the Lord and in the power of His might" (Ephesians 6:10).

REFLECTION AND DISCUSSION

1. What is the most blatant spiritual warfare you have ever personally seen?
2. What comes to mind when you think of having dominion? How conscious of this have you been? What have you been taught about it?
3. "Victory isn't the victory; faith is the victory." What are your thoughts and feelings about that?
4. "There are no official feelings of the power of God." What are your thoughts and feelings about that?
5. What does faith accomplish in 1 Corinthians 16:13?

CHAPTER 3
CASTING DOWN STRONGHOLDS

Be strong in the faith of this truth, make it an article of your creed; with the same faith you believe that there is a God, believe also this God's almighty power is thy sure friend.
~William Gurnall

BABY STEPS

For the weapons of our warfare are not carnal but mighty in God for pulling down strongholds, casting down arguments and every high thing that exalts itself against the knowledge of God, bringing every thought into captivity to the obedience of Christ. (2 Corinthians 10:4-5)

There's a great theological movie you might have seen, called *What About Bob?*

Bill Murray plays a lovable, obsessive guy named Bob. There's a great scene where Bob has to walk down a hallway from his therapist's office. He's got his pet fish with him.

Bob is so full of anxieties and phobias, he can barely function. Just to take this walk is an epic challenge. So he has to talk himself into it. You might remember what he keeps saying to get through it: "Baby steps. Baby steps down the hallway. Baby steps into the elevator…"

Baby steps.

To go from the ridiculous to the sublime, C.S. Lewis penned a classic book on spiritual warfare. It's called *The Screwtape Letters*. A junior demon writes a series of reports to a senior demon and hears back from the senior demon. The reports concern the junior demon's "subject"—the man he is supposed to influence away from God, truth, Jesus Christ, salvation, and an abundant life.

The senior demon keeps giving the same advice. He tells the junior demon above all else, *Never draw attention to yourself. Whatever you do, do it incrementally. Do it with subtlety. Do it with craft.*

Lewis writes, "Indeed the safest road to Hell is the gradual one—the gentle slope, soft underfoot, without sudden turnings, without milestones, without signposts."

You can say that the devil's plan to consume this man's life is to drag him away from God by baby steps.

This is what makes Satan so hard to spot and, therefore, so hard to resist.

He infiltrates minds slowly, slowly. Inch by inch. He persuades us to his way of thinking incrementally. Step by step. Imperceptibly. He puts our relationship with God on ice slowly. By degrees. Never drawing attention to himself.

A Christian devolves from a heartfelt child of God to a sincere questioner, to a doubter, to a skeptic, to a de-converter, to an avowed atheist, to an anti-Christian. It's all incremental. Baby steps. As their love of God wanes, their moral code evaporates too.

This is the warfare we are in. These are the wiles of the devil.

STRONGHOLDS

Strongholds are large, fortified structures in the human soul. They are ways of thinking, believing, and feeling that have come to live in your heart, sometimes without you realizing it.

Strongholds are psychological contraptions — engines in the soul — pieced together by Satan to manufacture fear, selfishness, anger, and every dark emotion. These strongholds infect everything with their toxic feelings and thoughts. They grow over time and can eventually run your life.

The devil hopes to keep these things hidden. But let's unmask them shall we?

Let's start by asking, How did they get there? How did something so big, so strong, so complex, so interconnected, and so destructive get into a person's soul? Where did the stronghold come from? Where did it start?

It started in Ephesians 4: "Be angry and do not sin: do not let the sun go down on your wrath, nor give place to the devil" (Ephesians 4:26-27).

That word "place" translates the Greek word *topos*. We get topology and topography from it.

Some translations say *foothold*. I like the word *turf*, like gang warfare.

Don't give up turf in your soul to the devil. Don't give a foothold, not even a toehold, in your soul—in your psychological makeup, in your beliefs, instincts, thoughts, or emotions—to the devil.

Here is the painful reality: *It is possible for you to give legal jurisdiction to the devil in your heart.*

Let that sink in.

So Scripture warns, "Neither give a foothold to the devil" (James 4:7). Why not?

Because the devil's strategy is to expand footholds into strongholds, and he will do it so slowly you don't even know it's happening.

> THE DEVIL'S STRATEGY IS TO EXPAND FOOTHOLDS INTO STRONGHOLDS, AND HE WILL DO IT SO SLOWLY YOU DON'T EVEN KNOW IT'S HAPPENING.

Never forget that in Scripture your foothold started with something as minor as going to bed angry.

We find the same thing in Hebrews, where the foothold is a root of bitterness—something as minor as holding onto a grudge, bitterness—that grows into a stronghold that short circuits grace in your life and actually "defiles many" (Hebrews 12:15).

Give the devil an inch and he'll take a mile. Give the devil a toehold, and soon he'll build a stronghold, a kind of mental nest, filled with screeching illusions, delusions, misconceptions, and self-deceptions, and all of it operated and fueled by evil spirits.

This whole mess does not start with a person forsaking God. It *ends* with forsaking God because it *starts* with something as small as a foothold.

And if all of that sounds bad, it is.

It is a plague. A spiritual and moral plague. It is the satanic battle plan to steal global dominion by capturing minds, and then hearts, and then lives, and then whole societies. Yes, it's bad.

But the promise of Scripture is that God is bigger, better, and stronger than anything Satan can do, and the weapons he provides are mighty in God to the casting down of strongholds. Just his little finger is a wrecking ball to every last one of these heartbreaking, life-sucking strongholds. With his weapons, you will win back any turf you surrendered. With his weapons you will rout the demons and make the devil flee.

That's the good news and that's the twenty-thousand foot view. Let's get into the details.

CASTING DOWN STRONGHOLDS

1. BATTLEFIELD: A stronghold is a structure of thinking that begins to dominate your mind.

Your mind is the battlefield. This is where the war is fought. It is the very real inner world of your mind, your heart, your psychology, and your soul.

So Satan works overtime to raise up strongholds across the battlefield of your mind.

- This wisdom does not descend from above, but is earthly, sensual, demonic. (James 3:15)
- Now the Spirit expressly says that in latter times some will depart from the faith, giving heed to deceiving spirits and doctrines of demons. (1 Timothy 4:1)
- But I fear, lest somehow, as the serpent deceived Eve by his craftiness, so your minds may be corrupted from the simplicity that is in Christ. (2 Corinthians 11:3)

The battlefield is the mind.

Whose truth will you believe? Whose truth will you base your life on? Whose truth will be the core of your decisions? Whose truth will you find at the center of your relationships, dating, marriage, and parenting?

Because if your core truth is not God's truth then it does not descend from above, and is earthly, sensual, and demonic.

Don't blame me, I'm just the messenger.

Every day is a battle over ideas:

- Truth vs. lies
- Reality vs. unreality
- Good vs. evil
- Doctrines of God vs. doctrines of demons
- Right vs. wrong
- Christ vs. other gods
- Christ vs. no god
- Christ vs. the prevailing mood of the culture
- The Bible vs. the philosophies of this age

So God warns, "Beware lest anyone take you captive through philosophy and empty deceit, according to the tradition of men, according to the basic principles of the world, and not according to Christ" (Colossians 2:8).

Your mind is a battlefield, and the devil wants to take you mentally captive, and by the way, he cheats.

2. MATRIX: A stronghold is hardened and enlarged when error connects with error and half-truths to form interlocking systems of self-reinforcing lies.

The devil's lies don't just float around in your brain as disconnected bad ideas. Instead, in your mind, the devil's lies actually come together. They actually form bigger lies.

> But there were also false prophets among the people, even as there will be false teachers among you, who will secretly bring in destructive heresies, even denying the Lord who bought them, and bring on themselves swift destruction. (2 Peter 2:1)

Destructive heresies are a system of teaching with enough truth to be attractive and enough untruth to be destructive.

Demonic error connects to demonic error which sucks in more

demonic error to form a network of interlocking, self-reinforcing matrix of lies.

They assemble entire systems, and philosophies, and structures. They pull together thoughts, ideas, arguments, truth-claims, instincts, emotions, opinions, and more. All these things get locked together like Legos on steroids.

They write books this way.

They teach university courses this way.

They develop complicated philosophies this way.

They make movies this way.

They seduce impressionable minds this way.

They go after opponents who don't swallow the pill this way.

Once the pieces of falsehood are locked together, these become Strongholds. Worldviews. Political parties. Global leaders. All of this is contaminated by the devil's spit.

Every stronghold is a matrix of error that occupies space in your soul, influences your choices, damages your emotions, and enlarges the turf of the devil.

All across the battlefield that is your mind, the devil is seeking to raise up these strongholds without you noticing.

3. DEFINITION: A stronghold is a mindset of defeat that causes me to accept as unchangeable a state of affairs that is contrary to the gracious promises of God.

A stronghold is an influential structure within a person's philosophy of life. It is your perception of the world as influenced by the dark side.

Let me break this one down.

A mindset of defeat... means that the devil has you convinced that the victories, the dreams, the prayers, the ideals that you hope for your life are out of reach. You are a loser. You are a victim.

This mindset of defeat causes you *to accept something as unchangeable*. This unchangeable quality is a dead giveaway. The devil wants you to believe that you are damaged goods and you will always be this way. It's unchangeable. Your damage is too deep, too big, too strong, too severe to ever find healing.

A stronghold is a mindset of defeat that causes me to accept as unchangeable *a state of affairs that is contrary to the gracious promises of God.* You see other people walking with God and enjoying his blessings, and you think, *That's not for me.* You hear of other people having their prayers answered and you think, *That's not for me.* You see other people find love and you think, *That's not for me.*

I want you to know that the voice of defeat, the voice of unchangeability, the voice that says you are severed from the grace of God—that is neither the voice of God nor of Scripture. It is the voice of the Wicked One, tossing toxins into the river of ideas flowing through your mind from the citadel of a demonic stronghold.

That voice is an infection. Only the Word of God by the Spirit of God can make it clean.

You've got to believe that all God's gracious promises are for you. I want you to find in this book the permission to declare that and believe it. I want you to to be able to say:

All the gracious promises of God are for ME.

- God's promise of an abundant life is for me. (John 10:10)
- God's promise of forgiveness is for me. (Ephesians 1:7)
- God's promise of peace that passes understanding is for me (John 10:27, Philippians 4:7)
- God's promise of joy unspeakable is for me. (1 Peter 1:8).
- God's promise that no weapon formed against you shall prosper is for me. (Isaiah 54:17)
- God's promise to work all things together for your good is for me. (Romans 8:28)
- God's promise to supply all your need is for me. (Philippians 4:19)

- God's promise to grant the desires of your heart is for me. (Psalm 37:4)
- God's promise to deliver from bondage and addiction and despair is for me. (Titus 2:14)
- God's promise that he is for you is for me. (Romans 8:31)
- God's promise that no one can stand against you is for me. (Romans 8:31)
- God's promise of mercy is for me. (Hebrews 8:12)
- God's promise of grace is for me. (2 Corinthians 9:8)
- God's promise of hope is for me. (1 Peter 1:3)
- God's promise of love is for me. (Jeremiah 31:3)
- All the gracious promises of God are for me. (2 Corinthians 1:20)

So we can be confident, "For all the promises of God in Him are Yes, and in Him Amen, to the glory of God through us" (2 Corinthians 1:20).

His promises are yours because they are Christ's and you are in Christ. So they are as much yours as they are Christ's. Do you believe?

Any voice that tells you otherwise is a liar.

A stronghold is a mindset of defeat that causes me to accept as unchangeable a state of affairs that is contrary to the gracious promises of God. But the truth is *all* the gracious promises of God are for me.

You need to be able to out-lawyer the devil, and when you keep on doing that, his strongholds will crumble to dust.

4. FALSE NORMAL: A stronghold is a satanic trick to create a false normal in your life.

I want to call out some strongholds right now. I'm not doing this to judge you or condemn you. That's not my heart.

I'm doing this out of compassion.

I'm doing this because you may have strongholds so deep and strong they feel normal to you, and you need somebody to to tell you that this isn't normal. This isn't the normal Christian life. This isn't God's plan for you. It's time to wake up and take hold of the weapons of your warfare.

See if you can find yourself in these strongholds:

- Drug use, drug addiction (sorcery), weed
- Alcoholism, getting drunk, partying
- Rage, temper, anger issues
- Relationship dysfunction
- Self-destructive tendencies, suicidal thoughts
- Eating disorders
- Bitterness, unforgiving spirit, revenge
- Arrogance, unteachable spirit
- Sexual addiction
- Sleeping around, shacking up, adultery, premarital sex
- Porn addiction
- Any sexual deviation from "one man, one woman, one lifetime"
- Gender dysphoria, gender denial
- Seduction, flirtatiousness
- False teaching, involvement in a cult
- Rebellion, divisiveness, disrespect of authority
- Assault, domestic violence, bullying
- Envy, coveting, jealousy
- Depression, despair, illness
- Fear, anxious thoughts, worry
- Prejudice, racism, sexism
- Liar, deception, hypocrisy, being a fake or a fraud
- Occultism, idol worship, witchcraft, horoscopes, ouija boards
- Theft, criminal behavior
- Laziness, sloth, entitlement to someone else's work

- Complaining, murmuring, negativity
- Gossip, slander, backbiting
- Obsession, compulsive thoughts/behaviors
- Unaddressed trauma
- Unhealthy vows, ungodly vows
- Can't receive love
- Legalism, religious spirit

When we move into this list, it's because we *think* we will find freedom or pleasure or joy. We might, but it's joy that doesn't last. In the end there's pain. These strongholds have brokenness and pain at the core.

Have you ever seen flies swarming to rotten meat?

Did you know that the Devil is the Lord of the Flies? That's one of his names in the Bible (Matt 12:24).

Because he swarms to wounds (strongholds) like flies to rotten meat. The festering wounds of a broken heart make easy prey for the devil.

Demonic strongholds try to make all of this feel normal, but it's a false normal. But it will never be normal for a child of God. That's because God loves you and wants better for you.

5. OBJECTIVE: Strongholds are engineered by Satan to steal your dominion, distort your freedom, and make you disobedient Christ's way of grace.

When you disobey Jesus again and again and again in the same area of sin, look for a stronghold. Chronic disobedience, chronic moral failure, a chronic bad attitude, and chronic disappointment with God are all flashing neon signs pointing to a stronghold in your heart.

You've been taken captive.

Your soul is made of mind, will, and emotions. This is your psyche, your identity, your psychology.

The devil infiltrates your mind and your emotions second, to take your will captive.

That way the choices you make that are supposed to be free will and are supposed to be byproducts of your God-given sovereignty instead have been "taken captive to do the devil's will."

St. Paul exhorts "that they may come to their senses and escape the snare of the devil, having been taken captive by him to do his will" (2 Timothy 2:26).

If a person has lost their senses, are they free?

If a person is in the snare of the devil, are they free?

If a person has been taken captive by Satan, are they free?

If a person is doing the will of Lucifer, are they free?

No, no, no, and no.

This person has been lured into a trap. They've been hypnotized. Anesthetized. Lulled to sleep by a diabolical lullaby from the Father of lies.

This is why strongholds have to be cast down. Not modified or compromised with or slightly adjusted.

We are talking about the casting down of strongholds. It is the only way to break free.

As I write, I am praying that you may come to your senses and escape the snare of the devil.

Now, how to do that? How to cast down strongholds?

Keep reading.

REFLECTION AND DISCUSSION

1. What have you heard about strongholds before?
2. What does this chapter say about strongholds that stands out for you?

3. What are some of the most *common* strongholds you see acting in people's lives? The most *powerful*? The most *damaging*?
4. Strongholds start as footholds. What do you feel and think about that?
5. What does Romans 1:21 say about the inner machinery of the human heart set in defiance against God?

CHAPTER 4
SIGNS OF A STONGHOLD

In a word, Christians, God and angels are spectators, observing how you quit yourselves like children of the Most High; every exploit your faith against sin and Satan causeth a shout in heaven.
~William Gurnall

DEMON POSSESSION

THERE'S an account in the gospels where Jesus goes to Peter's house. Peter's mother is sick, and Jesus heals her. Then we read this: "When evening had come, they brought to Him many who were demon-possessed. And He cast out the spirits with a word, and healed all who were sick" (Matthew 8:16).

This is not an antiquated, pre-scientific, outmoded way of thinking. It is not human reason, but divine revelation, that helps us know these things are so, and they are still happening today, and they are far more common than most of us realize.

There are four books in the Bible that describe the life, death, and resurrection of Jesus. These are called the Gospels—Matthew,

Mark, Luke, and John. In the gospels, one of the most frequent things Jesus did was to cast out evil spirits from people who are described as demon-possessed. There are over one hundred examples of this just in the Gospels.

Now this verse was originally written in Greek. There is a Greek word that has been translated *demon-possessed*. That is not a great translation of the Greek word, and many Bible experts are moving away from that term.

The word is simply *daimonizomai*. The first part does mean demon, an evil spirit. But the second part does not mean possessed. The word simply means *demonized*. Every time I see demon-possessed in my Bible, in my mind, I make it demonized.

I have been asked many times if a Christian can be demon-possessed. My answer is no, never, absolutely not, because to *possess* means to own, and every believer in Jesus Christ has been bought with a price, with the precious blood of Christ. If you are a Christian, you belong to God. He owns you. So no, a true child of God can never be "possessed" by evil spirits.

But that doesn't tell the whole story.

Because being demonized is a spectrum from very mild to very intense, and every act of demonization sits on that spectrum.

Scripture is very clear that demons are on the prowl for Christians today. So we are warned:

- Be sober, be vigilant; because your adversary the devil walks about like a roaring lion, seeking whom he may devour. (1 Peter 5:8)
- Put on the whole armor of God, that you may be able to stand against the wiles of the devil. For we do not wrestle [grapple] against flesh and blood, but against principalities, against powers, against the rulers of the darkness of this age, against spiritual hosts of wickedness in the heavenly places. (Ephesians 6:11-12)

- [L]est Satan should take advantage of us; for we are not ignorant of his devices. (2 Corinthians 2:11)
- I do not want you to have fellowship with demons. (1 Corinthians 10:20)
- Neither give place [a foothold] to the devil. (Ephesians 4:27)

I am saying this because many Christians have been told they cannot be demon-possessed, which is true, so they think that gives them a hall pass not to be concerned with spiritual warfare. That is untrue.

Even in this small sampling of verses, we discover:

- Satan still seeks whom he may devour.
- Satan can gain a foothold in our lives.
- Satan can grapple with us face to face.
- Satan can take advantage of us.
- Satan can lure us into fellowship, a partnership, with him.

As a pastor and Christian leader, I have a duty to warn you that even though you cannot be possessed by demons or the devil, you can be oppressed by them. You can be afflicted by them. You can be demonized to at least some degree. Demonic oppression exists on a spectrum.

I have talked to Christians, and I have known Christians, and I have ministered to true believers in the Lord who have been locked in a fierce battle with the dark side. It is serious business and no one is immune.

As I have already said, there is *victory* in the Lord Jesus Christ, and we are more than conquerors in his name. His shed blood and glorious resurrection are the reason we can pray, "Do not lead us into temptation, but go on delivering us from the Evil One." Scripture declares that and I've seen that and I know it to be true.

THE BLIND SPOT

If the devil has gained a foothold in your life, and grown that foothold into a stronghold, but all this feels normal, then how do you know it's happening?

Normal doesn't raise red flags.

Normal doesn't make you call for help or ask for prayer.

Everybody has a blind spot right where their stronghold is. Oh, we know that something's dramatically wrong, but we never associate it with spiritual warfare. We find an insurmountable problem/pain/dysfunction/evil in our hearts, but rationalize it. We explain it in naturalistic terms. We figure it's just bad luck, genetics, or our lot in life.

No.

It's an attack from the dark side. Wake up to your blind spots!

So how do you know there's a stronghold in your life that you need to cast down? How do you identify that you have a stronghold?

I want to give you nine warning signs of strongholds in your life. Nine ways you will feel if the dark side has taken turf on the battlefield of your mind.

I suggest you do a searching moral inventory using this list.

NINE WARNING SIGNS OF A STRONGHOLD

1. You feel TEMPTED.

A stronghold is always whispering to you that you should do something you know is wrong, unhealthy, or against your conscience. Remember the essence of temptation. All temptation is a suggested shortcut to the realization of a good goal. What shortcuts are you taking? They are pointers to strongholds.

James writes, "But each one is tempted when he is drawn away by his own desires and enticed" (James 1:14).

When you feel temptation to do that which is wrong, and your conscience starts flashing warning signs, but you feel you can't help yourself, and you give in over and over and over again, you might have a stronghold.

2. You feel HARASSED.

If a large portion of your life feels like troubles keep pecking at you and they never let up, you might have a demon-infested stronghold.

This stronghold changes your personality. When you have a stronghold of harassment, all the little things get to you. There are so many, that they add up.

So one more little problem hits you, and you overreact. But if someone could see the accumulation of all these little things, it's not overreaction, it makes sense. When this happens, you go into an altered state. You become cynical. Detached. Cocooned. Your spouse, family, and friends can see it happening. They see it in your eyes.

The devil harasses you with irritations and pessimism and unbelief and fears and anxieties and threats. There's simply no peace.

So therefore, there's a stronghold.

3. You feel TORMENTED

Demons are tormentors. "And He came down with them and stood on a level place with a crowd of His disciples and a great multitude of people… came to hear Him and be healed of their diseases, as well as those who were tormented with unclean spirits…"(Luke 6:17-18).

There are many different kinds of torment:

- Physical torment
- Mental torment
- Emotional torment
- Sexual torment
- Identity torment

God never meant for your life to feel like torture. Yes, this fallen world is a morally broken pain machine. But there's armor for that. There's armor that can take the hit. There's armor by which, even in the pain machine, you can thrive.

But torture? That's the devil's objective, not God's. That's a demonic stronghold, not a divine stronghold.

4. You feel COMPELLED.

Anything compulsive is a sign of a stronghold, of a demonic area of attack in a person's life. Where you feel out of control. Where you can't help yourself. Where your mind says no, but your will does it anyway.

It's a stronghold.

Paul describes it this way: "For what I am doing, I do not understand. For what I will to do, that I do not practice; but what I hate, that I do… But now, it is no longer I who do it, but sin that dwells in me" (Romans 7:15-17).

Wherever you've heard yourself saying, "I couldn't help myself. I couldn't help it." There you have a stronghold.

Wherever you find yourself triggered by certain things to do certain actions that are broken, there you have a stronghold.

I want to be very clear. There are genuine physiological and psychological roots of compulsion. I am not blaming you. I am not saying these things are your fault. I am saying that the devil takes advantage of these pre-existing conditions. Remember, he's a dirty opportunist. Therefore, even as you employ other therapeutic means for your healing, you also must not forget the spiritual battle you are in. In addition to therapies, remember to wear your armor. Remember to demolish your strongholds. Remember to pray and to receive prayer.

All addiction is a stronghold.

All dysfunction is a stronghold.

All compulsion is a stronghold.

Because a stronghold is Satan's attack on your dominion; his goal is to take you captive to do his will (2 Timothy 2:26).

5. You feel ENSLAVED.

You commit a sin, say a sexual sin. You confess your sin to God. You remember you are forgiven. You remember you are loved. You remember you are justified and clean before God.

But then, a minute later, you feel an overwhelming desire to do it again.

Scripture warns, "Do you not know that to whom you present yourselves slaves to obey, you are that one's slaves whom you obey, whether of sin leading to death, or of obedience leading to righteousness?" (Romans 6:16).

This stronghold makes you feel like you're losing control. Actually, you are, because the enemy has broken through the gates and stolen your dominion.

Who is the boss of you?

What force is running your life?

God made you to be free, and to feel free, but if you feel enslaved that's a sign of a stronghold.

6. You feel DIRTY.

You're doing stuff you promised God you would never do. You're crossing lines you thought you would never cross.

Your mind pictures things that would make you so ashamed if anybody found out.

Your heart feels emotions and rage and darkness that shock even yourself.

And no matter how many times you tell yourself you are forgiven, powerful, and clean you still feel defiled. That's a stronghold.

Jesus said, "For from within, out of the heart of men, proceed evil thoughts, adulteries, fornications, murders, thefts, covetousness, wickedness, deceit, lewdness, an evil eye, blasphemy, pride, foolishness. All these evil things come from within and defile a person" (Mark 7:21-23).

In this category, I include self-rejection, self-pity, and a victim mentality.

7. You feel REBELLIOUS.

I'm calling this what it is. When a Christian takes God's Word, and sets their own opinions above God's Word, that is rebellion, and it is something God warns against: "Today, if you will hear his voice, do not harden your hearts as in the rebellion" (Hebrews 3:15).

This stronghold is manifested when you harden your heart against God, and give yourself permission to go your own way instead of his way. When you give yourself permission to tell God he is wrong, it means you have already welcomed a pandoras box of gremlins inside the mentality of your soul.

Do you realize how many Christians have hardened their hearts against God so much, and disobeyed his word so much, that going to church, and reading the Bible, and serving God, and praying... all of that is becoming a tiny speck in the rearview mirror.

COVID has really sifted the church. Estimates say that one third of Christians have decided they are not coming back to church and therefore will not raise their kids in church. The reasons for this are many and complex, including a litany of failures by the church. As I see it, however, the essence of it is a refusal to submit to God. It is to join the rebels in Jesus's parable, who said, "We will not have this man to reign over us" (Luke 19:14). In my pastoral opinion: *Leaving church is the opiate of the immoral.* Yes, I know that's a provocative statement. Is it true? That's for the deconverters and deconstructionists to decide.

Scripture says, "Rebellion is as the sin of witchcraft" (1 Samuel 15:23). It is a stronghold of Satan.

This category includes the stronghold of pride. If you're thinking, wow, all those messed up people out there with all those strongholds, I thank God I'm not like them… There's your sign.

8. You feel HOPELESS/DESPERATE/DONE.

That spirit is not from God, "For God has not given us a spirit of fear, but of power and of love and of a sound mind" (2 Timothy 1:7).

I say this with all the tenderness and with all the firmness I can. I want you to know that any voice trying to drive you to end your life, or to destroy another life, or to do anything harmful to yourself or others, that voice is not from God.

It's not even from you.

You're being lied to. It is a voice from the dark side, a whisper of Satan, and it is a stronghold of demonic ideation that must and can be cast down with the mighty weapons of God.

There is another voice—the voice from heaven, the voice of truth—and this voice must grow louder.

It is constantly saying, "Don't give up, and never quit, because all things are possible with God."

9. You feel BITTERLY ANGRY.

There is holy anger and unholy anger. The unholy kind can become chronic. It's always there. Sometimes simmering. Sometimes blowing up.

We are therefore warned, "Looking carefully lest anyone fall short of the grace of God; lest any root of bitterness [unresolved anger] springing up cause trouble, and by this many become defiled" (Hebrews 12:15).

Unholy anger is displaced anger. You're mad at someone from your past, but taking it out on someone in your present.

Unholy anger is disproportionate anger. The punishment is too great for the crime.

Unholy anger is damaging anger, because it injures your relationships, it pushes away the people trying to love you, and it leeches your joy away.

This is a demonic stronghold.

This is that root of bitterness that defiles many. It is letting the sun go down on your wrath, opening up that foothold for the devil, and hanging on to the anger as the foothold becomes a stronghold.

NOT NORMAL

When you feel tempted, harassed, tormented, compelled, enslaved, dirty, rebellious, hopeless, or chronically angry—it means you've taken some hits in the battle. There is now a wound in your soul that the devil has taken advantage of. The demons are swarming like flies.

But you are oblivious to all of that because you think it's just normal.

It is not normal, not for you and not for anyone.

It is a wearisome, worrisome, unwholesome way of walking in this world.

But, I have very good news for you: "For the weapons of our warfare are not carnal but mighty in God for pulling down strongholds, casting down arguments and every high thing that exalts itself against the knowledge of God, bringing every thought into captivity to the obedience of Christ" (2 Corinthians 10:4-5).

Christian, you are a soldier of the Cross. You have weapons. You have armor to put on. In this armor you are invincible.

Without that armor, these strongholds make you a casualty. These strongholds let the Enemy of your soul into your soul and give him a base of operations.

By them, Satan either wounds you so deeply you need the MASH unit, or he distracts you so persistently you forget to fight the fight.

It's time to expel Satan from his influence over you, and time to tear down the strongholds.

When they brought to Jesus people who were demonized, he cast out the demons with a word. Because when the demons go, the strongholds crumble.

Jesus is still doing that today, so let's ask him to do it here, for us, right now.

Here is a prayer you can pray to begin to demolish your strongholds. In addition to this prayer, I recommend you ask your church leaders (elders) to anoint you with oil and pray for healing and deliverance in accordance with James 5:13-15. If you don't know what to pray for, think through the signs of a stronghold, and start there.

PRAYER

Dear Father
I come to you now for mercy and for strength.
Mercy to forgive my sins.
Strength to set me free.
You see the battle I am in, and you know where I have
  fallen down.

I confess to you, Lord God, that I have given the devil a foothold.

[Name a couple of areas where you have given in to temptation.]

Lord, I am sorry for these sins. I repent of these footholds and the sins that caused them.

And right now, I tear down every stronghold.

Specifically I cast down the Stronghold/s of... [name them here.]

I bring every thought into captivity that I may walk in obedience to Christ.

I turn away from bitterness and grudges.

I turn away from hatred.

I turn away from rebellion against you.

I renounce the devil and all his works. I turn away from all occult practices.

Now Lord, I come against any evil, and against any spirit in me that occupies any area of my personality.

I will not make peace with them.

I will not compromise with them.

I say they have no place in me.

And the only spirit I permit in my life is your Holy Spirit, dear God.

In the authority and power of Jesus and his shed blood, I tear down the strongholds. I command all other spirits to flee.

And I ask you Jesus, say the word, and set me free.

In Your Precious name,

Amen

REFLECTION AND DISCUSSION

1. Having read this chapter, what are your thoughts about the term "demon-possessed?"
2. What do you think demons can do to true Christians? What do you think they can't do?
3. How does it make you feel to think that strongholds actually become blind spots in our lives?
4. Of the nine signs of strongholds, which ones seem most relevant among your circle of friends? Which are most relevant in your life?
5. What does Galatians 5:1 tell you about the new normal for spiritually healthy believers?

CHAPTER 5
WHAT IS THE ARMOR OF GOD?

Heaven's way is paved with grace and mercy to the end.
~William Gurnall

THE WINDSWEPT HOUSE

THE GOSPEL of Luke tells of a time when Jesus was casting out demons. The legalistic religious rulers object to this action. They accuse Jesus of operating by the power of Beelzebub, which is another name for the devil.

Jesus takes religious rulers apart both logically and biblically.

He then offers two short parables, talking about spiritual warfare with the devil and his demons.

In the first parable, Jesus says, "When a strong man, fully armed, guards his own palace, his goods are in peace" (Luke 11:21).

In context, the Strong Man is Satan. Jesus has just encountered a heavily demonized man. The demons have taken a foothold and from it built a stronghold in his life. They are the heavily armed thugs. Satan is the strong man; his demons are squatters in the man's soul.

Satan is armed with his power and his wiles, with ignorance, with error, with unbelief, and with pride.

He keeps guard over his palace. Once in possession of a human heart, or of any corner of a human heart, he does all he can to tighten his grip on it.

Jesus says, "his goods are in peace." All is well, from Satan's perspective. This is the messed up kind of "peace" in the heart of a person who has turned against God. They have a good opinion of themselves. They flatter themselves. They justify themselves. Worst of all, they settle for a normal that isn't normal.

A sub-normal *status quo* is the dirtiest trick in the devil's playbook.

Jesus paints this picture of a spiritual casualty: a person whose heart, soul, and mind are captivated by the Strong Man, Satan, and bewitched by a stronghold of darkness. Such a person stoops beneath a burden of sadness and despair.

They are all too common in our world today. They are even common in our churches.

But here comes Jesus with his second parable: "But when a stronger than he comes upon him and overcomes him, he takes from him all his armor in which he trusted, and divides his spoils" (Luke 11:22).

The Strong Man is dangerous and fierce. But thank God for the Stronger Man, Jesus Christ. He is the Mighty God. All power is given unto him in heaven and on earth.

When he flexes his muscles, Satan and his thugs turn tail and scurry off as fast as their diabolical legs can carry them.

Jesus Christ is stronger than the Strong Man. Far stronger. He has already put a beating on the Strong Man, already triumphed over him, already sealed his doom, already crushed his head, already broken his back, already proven his lie, already demolished his pride.

In his parable, Jesus, the Stronger Man, takes from Satan, the Strong Man, "all his armor in which he trusted."

Jesus is saying that the devil has his own kind of armor! What is Satan's armor? What are the weapons of *his* warfare?

Unfortunately, his weapons would be all too familiar to most of us. They include: the fear of death, temptation, hatred, lust, depression, brainwashing, secularism, humanism, idol worship, addiction, dysfunction, deception, delusion, hopelessness, disobedience, and more.

All these forces are from the dark side.

But whatever tools fill the Satanic tool belt, when the Stronger Man exerts his power, Satan's tools are nullified. Jesus takes away the Strong Man's armor.

> "Having disarmed principalities and powers, He made a public spectacle of them, triumphing over them in [the power of the Cross]." (Colossians 2:15)

Jesus, by his Cross, disarmed the principalities and powers.

In the war for our souls, Jesus takes possession of the citadel of the heart and drives out the usurper.

The weapons Jesus used in his warfare are mighty through God.

Now, he has given us those very same weapons! He invites us to use them. They will continue to disarm and drive out demonic influence wherever it rears its insidious head.

Then Jesus continues his parable of the Strong Man with this: "He who is not with Me is against Me, and he who does not gather with Me scatters" (Luke 11:23).

He is saying there is no neutral ground.

I will come back to this, because it will make more sense when we look at the very next mini-parable by Jesus.

> "When an unclean spirit goes out of a man, he goes through dry places, seeking rest; and finding none, he says, 'I will return to my

house from which I came.' And when he comes, he finds it swept and put in order. Then he goes and takes with him seven other spirits more wicked than himself, and they enter and dwell there; and the last state of that man is worse than the first." (Luke 11:24-26)

It's not enough to evict the bad guys. If you don't put something in their place, the bad guys come back, and things become worse than before.

The house may be swept out, but it hasn't been filled yet. It may be put in order, but it's not occupied by the Lord Jesus Christ.

Nature abhors a vacuum, and so it is in the spiritual realm. *Something* will fill that vacuum.

THE DANGERS OF THE UNFILLED HEART

1. THE VACUUM: When you pull down demonic strongholds you create a vacuum, so you have to build up something in their place.

The biblical word for that vacuum is *vanity*. It means emptiness or a vacuum. This is the Greek word *mataiotes*, which is typically translated vanity or futility

So Paul warns against the "vanity of the mind" (Ephesians 4:17). He knows that a vacuum always draws in something, and in the spiritual realm that *something* will be fed in from the dark side.

In the natural realm, everything seems great and in order. But in the spiritual realm, there is a vacuum that is drawing in the doctrines of demons.

These are people who have been genuinely saved, walked with the Lord, and then dropped out.

Dropped out of church.

Dropped out of worship and prayer.

No more quiet time. No genuine prayer. No dedication to sitting under the preaching of the Word of Christ. No Christian service, and no meaningful walk with God.

But everything else is fine.

The house is swept. The house is put in order. No really gross sins. They say things like, "Well, I'm not out killing people." Do you know how many times someone has said that to me?

Way to set the bar high! That's an amazing Christian life—you're not killing anybody. Well done!

Yes, a very fine neat and tidy house you've got there, in the natural realm.

But spiritually speaking, you're empty. There is a vacuum in your soul. A dangerous emptiness within. Yes, you are saved. Yes, you are going to heaven. Yes, it is impossible to lose your salvation. As I've already said, no true believer can ever be possessed by demons or the devil. But your thoughts can be so distorted and so twisted that the wonders of salvation have become a receding memory in the rearview mirror. Peter talks about people who "have forgotten they have been cleansed from their old sins" (2 Peter 1:9).

They are truly cleansed.

They have truly forgotten their cleansing.

Mentally and psychologically speaking, they have emptied their memories of amazing grace, which is dangerous because the devil and demons are standing by to fill that spiritual emptiness again and to rebuild whatever dark strongholds you've torn down.

2. THE DANGER: In the spiritual realm, it's not enough to subtract the bad stuff. You have to add in the good stuff, or the bad stuff comes back with a vengeance.

In this same context, Jesus said, "He who is not with me is against me. He who does not gather with me scatters" (Luke 11:23).

This means that a deactivated Christian is in great danger. The one who is not with Jesus *is against* him. The one who does not gather with Jesus *scatters*. This person has set themselves in opposition to the mission of Jesus.

That is an epic invitation to trouble. In the spiritual realm, it's not enough to subtract the bad stuff. You have to add in the good stuff, or the bad stuff comes back with a vengeance.

I am talking about genuine believers in Jesus. They are saved. They are going to heaven. Yet, they are casualties in the angelic conflict, and strangers from the full experience of the blessing of God. They are prisoners of war in their minds, in their emotions, and in their wills (2 Timothy 2:26).

They've done the first part of 2 Corinthians 10:4,5, but have stopped short of doing the second part.

> For the weapons of our warfare are not carnal but mighty in God for pulling down strongholds, casting down arguments and every high thing that exalts itself against the knowledge of God, *bringing every thought into captivity to the obedience of Christ*. (2 Corinthians 10:4-5)

If you've started to tear down strongholds, that's fantastic. God is working in you. But don't skip the part where we bring every thought into captivity to the obedience of Christ. Because it's time to understand there is another kind of stronghold in the Word of God.

3. THE BETTER STRONGHOLD: The armor of God is a divine stronghold, a machine in the soul to bring you into your inheritance.

It's not enough to just tear down satanic strongholds. We also have to faithfully build up divine strongholds if we expect to stand strong in the Lord. This is the armor of God. View it as the stronghold you always wanted!

- The LORD is my rock and my fortress and my deliverer; My God, my strength, in whom I will trust; My shield and the horn of my salvation, my stronghold. (Psalm 18:2)
- The LORD is good, A stronghold in the day of trouble; And He knows those who trust in Him. (Nahum 1:7)
- The name of the LORD is a strong tower; The righteous run to it and are safe. (Proverbs 18:10)
- Be my strong refuge, To which I may resort continually; You have given the commandment to save me, For You are my rock and my fortress. (Psalm 71:3)
- "I will say of the LORD, "He is my refuge and my fortress; My God, in Him I will trust." (Psalms 91:2)

We tear down strongholds that are demonic, so that we can build up strongholds that are divine.

This is where the armor of God comes in.

So what is the armor of God? I've been puzzling over this for a while. What is the armor of God. It's not literal armor. It's a metaphor. But a metaphor for what?

All the pieces of armor fit together. It's a system. A matrix. The pieces snap together like pieces in a Lego set.

In other words, the armor of God is another kind of stronghold.

The Armor of God is a *divine* stronghold to replace and displace the *demonic* strongholds of Satan.

So Paul gives us a list with six pieces of armor. These are taken from the armor of a Roman soldier. St Paul, who made this list, is very familiar with this, because he was in Roman custody on his way to trial before Caesar. He saw these soldiers all day long. He saw them put on and take off their armor countless times.

Here are the six plus one pieces of armor.

- The Belt
- The Breastplate

- The Boots
- The Shield
- The Helmet
- The Sword
- Prayer

Each piece represents a set of interlocking structures of biblical truth. The Belt represents Truth. The Breastplate represents Righteousness. The Boots represent the Preparation of the Gospel. The Shield represents Faith. The Helmet represents Salvation. The Sword represents the Spirit's weapon, which is the Word of God. Prayer represents itself.

What are we talking about?

The armor of God is not a magic spell. It is not a bunch of words to declare if you're scared of the devil.

These are not magical words. This is not superstition.

Each piece of armor is a whole way of thinking. A mindset.

- A mindset of truth to understand reality and weed out delusions.
- A mindset of righteousness to understand the moral rectitude of God and his ways of aligning you to it.
- A mindset of the Gospel as both your mission and your hope.
- A mindset of faith, so that you will believe what God says is true enough to act like it.
- A mindset of salvation, so that every thought you entertain is filtered through the power of the Cross.
- A mindset of the Word of God, to drive back the darkness and bring in the light.
- All of which is cemented and mortared together by prayer.

Each divine mindset locks together with each other mindset, and all together you have a stronghold in the Lord.

So the Bible speaks of strongholds of Satan and of a stronghold of God. This is the building project of your life.

THE FIRST SONG

When we opened our church's new worship center, we held a dedication ceremony. We worshiped, we prayed, we declared Scripture, and we dedicated our building to God for the glory of Christ and the propagation of the Gospel.

The first song ever sung in our sanctuary was chosen with great intention. *We sang A Mighty Fortress is Our God.* That is not an easy song to sing. It has an awkward melody. The rhythm is uneven. It really needs a giant pipe organ so loud it rumbles your chest.

It's very hard to sing and play with a contemporary worship band.

Even so, I picked it on purpose for a lot of reasons.

First, I wanted to establish our church, and our mission, on the great historical foundations of biblical Christianity. We are rooted in 2,000 years of Christian witness and martyrdom.

Second, I wanted to ensure that our church would always be about pressing the battle against Satan. That we would not be content coasting, resting, or growing complacent. I wanted our church to always be a battleship, not a cruise ship.

Third, I picked that hymn because I wanted to set us all squarely on the victory that is Jesus Christ. In this great battle of the ages, we don't fight *for* victory, we fight *from* victory.

When I was a freshman at Wheaton College, I had a professor who made us memorize this hymn.

Please enjoy those truly epic lyrics:

> *A mighty fortress is our God, a bulwark never failing;*
> *Our helper he, amid the flood of mortal ills prevailing.*

THE CHRISTIAN IN COMPLETE ARMOR   67

For still our ancient foe doth seek to work us woe;
His craft and power are great, and armed with cruel hate,
On earth is not his equal.

Did we in our own strength confide, our striving would be losing,
Were not the right Man on our side, the Man of God's own choosing.
You ask who that may be? Christ Jesus, it is he;
Lord Sabaoth his name, from age to age the same;
And he must win the battle.

And though this world, with devils filled, should threaten to undo us,
We will not fear, for God has willed his truth to triumph through us.
The prince of darkness grim, we tremble not for him;
His rage we can endure, for lo! his doom is sure;
One little word shall fell him.

That Word above all earthly powers no thanks to them abideth;
The Spirit and the gifts are ours through him who with us sideth.
Let goods and kindred go, this mortal life also;
The body they may kill: God's truth abideth still;
His kingdom is forever!

This is a mature hymn of the Church. Those lyrics serve up solid meat for grownups—provision for loyal warriors of the Cross. If you're going to war, you need a song like this.

Ask yourself a question: Is God truly your mighty fortress?

Because this is your great potential as a Child of God.

God can be your bulwark never failing.

God can become your helper amid the flood of ills, and difficulties, and hardships, and frustrations, and bad things happening in your life, in the middle of all that, prevailing.

When you run into your mighty fortress, you will not fear, for God has willed that *his truth* will triumph through you.

When you've made God your fortress, you do not tremble over that grim prince of darkness.

You do not tremble; you can endure his rage, he can hit you with his best shot, and you will not be moved because God has become *your* Mighty Fortress: your refuge, your strength, your stronghold in the day of trouble, your rock, your fortress, your deliverer, and your strong tower.

This is the call of God on your life. This is the main thing—that you will build in your own soul this invincible stronghold, an unshakable sense of the power and presence of God.

This is the stronghold you need.

This is the stronghold you actually construct, brick by brick, as you put on the armor of God again and again and again, going deeper and deeper as you go.

Now, let's study our supernatural armor piece by piece.

PRAYER

Almighty God, today, I put on the full armor of God.
I put on the BELT OF TRUTH, to understand the times in
   which I live.
I put on the BREASTPLATE OF RIGHTEOUSNESS, to
   guard and protect my heart.
I put on the BOOTS OF THE GOSPEL, for my mission in
   a hurting world.
I take up the SHIELD OF FAITH, to believe my God no
   matter what.

*I wear the HELMET OF SALVATION, to guard my mind
from delusion and despair.
I carry the SWORD OF THE SPIRIT, to defeat the darkness and lift high the Cross.
I declare myself a soldier of the Cross.
I stand in the Victory of Christ.
I make you, God, my stronghold today.
Amen.*

REFLECTION AND DISCUSSION

1. What evidence, if any, do you see of the Strong Man (Satan's) influence among your circle of friends? among the unsaved people in your world?
2. What do you think and feel about the idea that the devil loves a vacuum in the human soul?
3. Why would we call the Armor of God another kind of stronghold? If the Armor of God is a divine stronghold, how is it formed? How is it put together? What are the materials from which it is made?
4. "The Armor of God is not a magic spell." How do you react to this? Why do you think it's important to say this?
5. According to 2 Timothy 3:16, 17 what would be some benefits of a stronghold constructed of truths from God's Word?

CHAPTER 6
THE BELT OF TRUTH

The Christian is bred by the Word, and he must be fed by it.
~William Gurnall

START HERE

"Stand therefore, having girded your waist with truth…" (Ephesians 6:14)

The Belt of Truth is the first and main piece of armor that holds everything else in place. As we've seen, the armor of God in the Bible is based on the armor of a Roman soldier in biblical times.

The belt was not like what we think of as a belt today. It was several inches wide. It was made of tough leather. It covered the soldier's whole stomach and all they way around the back. It protected the soldier's whole midsection.

When soldiers geared up, the belt was the first thing they put on.

The reason it was first was because everything else attached to the belt one way or another. There was a scabbard to hold the sword and connection to lock in the bottom of the breastplate. There were hooks to help hold up the shield, hooks and pockets for armor, knives, and food, and a leather pouch for drinks.

Not only that, the belt kept soldiers from tripping over their clothes. It held their tunics tight, so nothing got in the way.

You could say that the Roman belt was the main piece of armor that held everything else in place.

When St. Paul instructs us on how to prepare for conflict—and for all of life's stresses—the one supernatural weapon that best matches this all-important belt is *truth*.

"Having girded your waist with truth."

If you're going to stand against the devil, if you're going to push back the darkness in your life and your world, if you're going to be a champion and not a casualty in the great conflict of the ages, if you're going to step into the confidence, the wholeness, the deliverance and everything else Jesus gained for you by his cross, then you have to start here.

Truth. Stand, having girded your waist with truth.

WHAT IS TRUTH?

What exactly is this truth we should buckle on every single day?

One of the longest running debates in philosophy is What is Truth. How do we find it? Where do we get it? What is its source?

Here is a biblical definition of truth.

> **Truth is reality as experienced, created, seen, and revealed by God.**

Both the Hebrew (*emeth*) and Greek (*aletheia*) words for truth indicate that which is solid, substantial, and real. Truth is bedrock reality. Like it or not, you can't defy truth and get away with it. You can't break God's truth. You can only break yourself by bashing yourself against God's truth.

Welcome to the real world.

I'm not going to try to defend or prove that definition right now. This book isn't the place for that. If you want to be technical, this understanding is called the Theistic Correspondence Theory of Truth. You can Google it if you want to.

Truth is reality.

Let's think through what this definition means.

TRUTH IS REALITY, THEREFORE...

1. This means that the deepest truths start outside of us.

You are not the source of truth. I am not the source of truth. God is the source of truth. God himself is the ultimate reality check.

If you want to find truth, don't look inside your heart; you have to look up and out to God. You have to look outside yourself first. You have to look to God's reality and to God's heart.

All of the everyday realities we experience and see actually exist independently of us. They're real. I'm real. You're real.

This includes the universe God has made. It includes its laws and all its motions. This includes the fact of your own existence. All these truths and more originate in external, objective realities created by God. They do not originate in your mind. Neither you, nor I, nor any other human invented these things.

You do not define truth, God defines truth.

You do not define reality, God defines reality.

You do not define me, God defines me.

You do not define yourself, God defines you.

This also calls into question the radical position that has now gone mainstream. That is the misguided notion that says you have your truth and I have my truth.

When engineers calculated the size of the I-beams for the roof trusses in our church's worship center, I really hope they didn't look within to their own truth to do the math. I hope they looked without to externally calculated charts showing the tensile strength of steel relative to the span of the roof. The "my truth, your truth" thing simply can't work in the real world.

If truth is reality as experienced, created, seen, and revealed by God, then the source of truth is outside of us, and we have to submit our opinions to that source, which is God. Anything contrary is actually a kind of rebellion.

When Scripture says to buckle on the belt of truth, it is telling you to see your life as God sees it and to see your world as God sees it.

To buckle on the belt of truth is to attune your whole being to reality.

Truth holds everything else together. Everything connects to truth, one way or another. Paul calls you to buckle on reality, to buckle on truth, so that you can see your life in crystal clarity, so that you can stand against the *wiles*—meaning the unrealities spewed forth—of the devil.

Truth makes sense of your intellectual world.

Truth makes sense of your moral world.

Truth makes sense of your spiritual world.

Truth makes sense of your emotional and psychological world.

Truth enables you to live without deception, evasion, or distortion.

The deepest truths start outside of us, because truth is reality as experienced, created, seen, and revealed by God.

If you go to any secular university, they will laugh at all this. Actually, they will attack it.

They will say that truth isn't objective (outside of you), it is subjective, meaning your truth and my truth are both true, even if they contradict.

The problem is simply that if there is no outside, external reference point for truth, then all we're left with is radical self-ism, with no values but what we invent, and no moral code but survival of the fittest.

The inevitable consequence of this is narcissism. Rampant narcissism. Welcome to today's decayed version of Western Civilization.

When the devil plotted the downfall of our culture, he started in the exalted halls of academia. He started with flocks of over-educated philosophers who argued there is no truth and then followed that out to conclude God is dead.

Truth doesn't matter, they said. What matters is feelings.

Now look at the mess we're in.

But truth does matter. Because of the most important things in life.

2. Truth matters because love matters.

As Christians, we are committed to truth. We believe it comes from God, through his Word, to us.

So we learn the truth. We live the truth. We stand for truth. We fight for truth with respect and grace.

Why? Because for us Christians, the fight for truth is not about winning a battle; it's not about proving ourselves right and everyone else wrong.

Rather, we fight for truth because the battle for truth is a battle for love.

3. Truth matters because love matters. You can't have love without trust, and you can't have trust without truth.

If you're in a relationship with someone, and they're not telling the truth to you, that hurts.

You're not going to trust them. You're going to keep your shields up. Your relationship will suffer.

Truth matters because love matters. No truth, no trust. No trust, no love. "Therefore, putting away lying, 'let each one of you speak truth with his neighbor,' for we are members of one another" (Ephesians 4:25).

Truth is the glue the holds relationships together and makes love possible.

The devil hates human flourishing. Wrecking human lives makes Satan happy, because he knows it is God's desire to bless us. What better strategy could the devil have than to destroy human flourishing by wrecking love, and what better way could he wreck love than by wrecking the truth that makes love possible?

Put on the belt of truth, love one another in grace and truth, and stand against the wiles of the devil by standing on God's truth.

3. Satan attacks truth to damage our lives and to drive a wedge between us and God.

Satan and the demons tear at truth like vultures on road kill.

Since the Garden of Eden, when the serpent tempted Eve, the main thing the devil does is undermine reality. He's sneaky and subtle, and he cheats.

Jesus called the devil a liar and the father of lies (John 8:44).

If you don't wear the belt of truth, you're going to be sucked into Satan's lies.

Here's a really important Bible verse from a super readable translation: "Don't let the world around you squeeze you into its mold, but let God re-mold your minds from within…" (Romans 12:2, Phillips)

Yes, the world is squeezing us into its mold, all the time.

But when you read the word "world" don't just think about culture. The world, in this sense, has a really dark side.

- "We know that we are of God, and the whole world lies under the sway of the Wicked One." (1 John 5:19)

- "Do you not know that friendship with the world is hostility with God? Whoever therefore wants to be a friend of the world makes himself an enemy of God." (James 4:4)
- "Now is the judgment of this world; now the ruler of this world [Satan] will be cast out." (John 12:31)

When Scripture says to not let the world around you squeeze you into its mold, *world* has a very specific and very demonic meaning.

The World, by definition, is the prevailing philosophies of a culture in rebellion against God, under the influence of Satan.

That world. That evil world. That demonically influenced world. Don't let that world squeeze you into its mold.

It is hard, because this is where we live, work, play, study, and hang out with friends.

We need to buckle on truth—a massive helping of truth—so that we can walk in reality and not be neutralized by the devil.

PROBLEM

I was listening to two pastors talk about what's going on with Gen Z and younger generations today. They ran through a list of ten moral and spiritual problems with younger generations.

These included father issues, a melting down of truth, a crisis in knowledge, a shift from a culture of authority to a culture of authenticity, digital distraction, and misdefined freedom. These also included the delusion that says there are no facts, only interpretations. These include a sinful desire for autonomy, skepticism toward the Bible among Christians, and the fear of being cancelled.

I think that's a great list.

The speakers then condensed it all down into one thing, and this is where I'm going to disagree, just a little, and make a change to what they said. They said that all these issues boiled down to *an authority problem with God.*

That is so true.

People have a basic refusal to submit to the rule and reign of God, so they perform all kinds of mental gymnastics to rationalize their refusal to submit.

It's a giant authority problem.

Yes it is.

But I think it's deeper than that, and if we're going to reach younger generations with the gospel, we have to understand this.

The real tragedy of a generation raised in our post-Christian, post-modern society isn't just an authority problem. That is a symptom of a deeper problem.

It's a reality problem.

The deepest problem today is not with authority, *it's with* reality.

For so many people today, there's nothing solid, there's nothing real, there's nothing true.

Along came postmodernism to rip away truth from underneath our feet. So we're not grounded on anything. There's no anchor. There's nothing solid, nothing dependable.

In 2014, the *Oxford English Dictionary* said that the word of the year is "post-truth." We live in a post-truth era, they say. That's like saying we live in a "post-gravity" era. But humans cannot function for long in "truthlessness" any more than we can function for long in weightlessness.

Truthlessness is a very scary way to live. And that's what postmodernism has given us, by design.

Then add in secularism. Secularism says there is no God, no heaven, no angels, no supreme being, nothing above us.

Postmodernism ripped away the floor, so there's nothing real below us to anchor us.

Secularism ripped away heaven, so there's nothing real above us to inspire us or give us hope. There's no meaning but what we invent. There's no sacredness to us, no creation in the image of God. Nothing transcendent toward which we can aspire. Nothing eternal. The only causes left to us are earthbound—environmentalism, sexual liberation, utopianism, and a host of social issues—all of which represent a new paganism, and all of which fall short of the human heart's sacred quest for our infinite Creator God. Our origin, they say, was the Big Bang, and our destiny, they say, is our snuffing out in death, and the cosmic heat death of maximum entropy. That this secular framework is adopted with religious fervor is one of Satan's crowning achievements.

So there's no truth beneath us and no transcendence above us, so we're just floating with no purpose, no direction, no meaning, and no joy.

It's absolutely depressing.

This may sound like abstract philosophy, but it's the concrete reality for a whole generation. All of this is playing out in an epidemic of sadness, cynicism, despair, suicide, and pain.

To take away truth is to take away reality. To take away reality is to take away trust. To take away trust is to take away love. To take away love is to plunge a person, a society, or a world into a frantic search for happiness that is ultimately futile.

This is the devil's endgame!

The devil said to Eve in the Garden of Eden four words: *has God indeed said* (Genesis 3:1)? Then he said, "You shall not die," a direct defiance against God's stated reality that proved to be all too real.

Satan keeps on asking this same question for all the long ages of time. He is calling truth itself into question. That is what we are seeing everywhere today.

It's the same thing that was happening 2,000 years ago, when a brilliant writer and thinker named Paul said to take up the Belt of Truth.

THE BELT

The Belt of Truth is your starting point to walk in victory in the great spiritual conflict of the ages.

The Bible is armor for your soul. It is the principal weapon of your warfare. In an event called the Temptation, Jesus hit Satan in the face by quoting Scripture four times (Matthew 4:4, 6, 7, 10). We should do the same.

We urgently need to know the deep things of God. We need theology. We need doctrine. We need to grasp the rich vocabulary of faith. We need meat, not milk. We need expository teaching and preaching. We need to push away from the kiddie table and join the grown ups at a feast of abundant and deep biblical truth.

> "For everyone who partakes only of milk is unskilled in the Word of Righteousness, for he is a babe. But solid food belongs to those who are of full age, that is, those who by reason of use have their senses exercised to discern both good and evil." (Hebrews 5:13-14)

By every account, there is an epidemic of biblical illiteracy in the Church today. No wonder the devil is eating us for lunch. No wonder we see a growing number of de-conversions and a theological cluelessness among Christians.

The devil seeks whom he may devour, and ignorant Christians make easy prey.

Churches exist, said Paul, "that we should no longer be children, tossed to and fro and carried about with every wind of doctrine, by the trickery of men, in the cunning craftiness of deceitful plotting" (Ephesians 4:14).

When Scripture tells you to put on the Belt of Truth, it is telling you the starting point for victory in the great spiritual conflict.

Start here with the Word of God.

Stay here in the Word of God.

Read your Bible. Get into a church dedicated to teaching it in depth. Find a good, Bible-teaching, grace-oriented pastor and keep showing up—for a lifetime. Get hungry for doctrine.

You've been infected by lies. Cleanse out the infection with "the washing of water by the Word" (Ephesians 5:26).

Here is the Belt of Truth.

Put it on, every single day.

REFLECTION AND DISCUSSION

1. What evidence do you see for the claim we live in a post-truth era?
2. How can having an "authority problem" be rooted in having a "truth problem?"
3. How would you rate yourself on your knowledge of Scripture? Of theology? How mighty is your Belt of Truth? What will you do to grow in this regard?
4. Where do you go for good Bible teaching? Are you raising your kids, leading your family, or guiding yourself into the deep things of God? Do you care? Do a searching moral inventory over your appetite for the deep truths of God.
5. What diagnosis does Hebrews 5:12 offer for believers who are not devoted to God's Word?

CHAPTER 7
THE BREASTPLATE OF RIGHTEOUSNESS, PART 1

Fear is Satan's weapon held in reserve. When alluring temptations fail, he opens his quiver and shoots these arrows to set the soul on fire, if not with sin then with terror. When he cannot carry a soul laughing to hell through the deception of pleasurable temptations, he will try to make him go mourning to heaven by this amazing attack. It is a sure sign that Satan is losing.
~William Gurnall

GUARD YOUR HEART

"Stand therefore… having put on the breastplate of righteousness…" (Ephesians 6:14)

The "breastplate" was a piece of armor that covered the chest and back of the soldier. Some breastplates were made of thick, hardened pieces of leather or even thick cloth. This was shaped to fit the warrior's upper body.

To make it stronger, manufacturers would cover the leather with something like roofing shingles, made of overlapping, thin slices of animal hooves, horns, or pieces of metal.

Other breastplates were made of large pieces of metal that were hammered to fit the warrior's body.

Regardless of the kind of breastplate the warrior wore, the function was the same.

The breastplate protected the heart.

In biblical days, they didn't have a vocabulary word for psychology. They didn't have a separate word for emotions. But they knew where you felt emotions, and it's the same as us today.

Where do you feel your deepest feelings? In your *gut*. In your *heart*. In the *pit of your stomach*.

The language the biblical authors used to describe emotional states had to do with organs in the thorax. For example, the Bible talks about being constricted in your *kidneys* (reins) and your *liver*. It talks about your *bowels*. It talks about your *flesh*. All of these things are bodily organs, and, when used of emotional or psychological states, none of these things is to be taken literally (meaning physiologically).

Not coincidentally, the Greek word translated *breastplate* is literally *thorax*.

When the Bible talks about your heart, which is a physical organ, it is referring mainly to an emotional state. In fact, we have used *heart* so much for the emotions that we hardly even think of the physical organ any more.

When Paul looked for a piece of armor that would protect a believer's emotional state—and actually your whole psychological condition—he choose the breastplate.

YOUR PSYCHE IS UNDER ATTACK

The biblical word *psyche* is usually translated *soul*. This is the basis of the English word *psychology*—the study of the soul. When the

Bible talks about your *psyche,* it means the interplay of your mind, will, and emotions.

If the devil can mess you up here, he has you where he wants you. This makes wearing your breastplate extremely important.

1. WARNING: The demons and the devil mount a relentless attack against your emotional and psychological health as a child of God.

Therefore, we should not go anywhere, either online or in real life, without having put on the breastplate.

I am not saying that *all* mental or psychological illness is demonic in origin. Not at all. There are many factors that go into the condition of our soul, including physiology, life experiences, and genetics.

But, this fallen world is a morally broken pain machine, and the devil is a cheater and an opportunist. Where there is an opening, he takes a foothold. Where he takes a foothold, he makes a stronghold. Where he makes a stronghold, there is sadness, "stuckness," sorrow, and pain.

Emotional brokenness is a favorite tactic of Satan.

Christian, you have an enemy. Your enemy plays dirty. Your enemy is a liar. Your enemy is a seducer. And your enemy will do whatever it takes to bring down your emotional health.

2. OBJECTIVE: If Satan gets his way, he'll make you psychologically broken.

The Word of God highlights the importance of your *mind*—the reservoir of thoughts and beliefs underlying your consciousness. The devil attacks your thinking, your ideas, your worldview, and your ideation. The central battlefield is the mind, and the lies of Satan will bring you down.

It's not just the *mind* that Satan attacks. He goes after your *emotions* too. He wants you to be psychologically immobilized.

I want to show you this in Scripture. It's the kind of truth that is hiding in plain sight. It's hard to see at first, but once you see it, you can't miss it. The author of Hebrews explains one of the purposes of the Cross when he writes, "That through death He might destroy him who had the power of death, that is, the devil, and release those who through fear of death were all their lifetime subject to bondage" (Hebrews 2:14-15).

The phraseology of this verse takes us deep into biblical psychology. He mentions *fear* and, specifically, *the fear of death*. He talks about being *subject to bondage*, which is biblical phraseology for addiction and dysfunction.

Scripture announces that work of Jesus Christ is God's way of stomping the devil on his head like the giant cockroach he is. Calvary's Cross releases those who believe from the psychological bondage of fear.

When the Bible speaks of slavery and bondage, about half the time it means literal slavery, like the Jews in Egypt.

But the other half the time it means emotional bondage, for example: "While they promise them liberty, they themselves are slaves of corruption; for by whom a person is overcome, by him also he is brought into bondage" (2 Peter 2:19).

This is another verse about human psychology. Here, *slaves of corruption* is once again biblical terminology for addiction and dysfunction.

All of that is called being *brought into bondage*.

We don't see the psychological wisdom of Scripture, because we're simply not accustomed to how the biblical authors speak of these things.

The devil wages a massive Psy-Ops campaign (psychological operations)—these things are part of the devil's diabolical arsenal to cause you to live in defeat.

Paul warns us about the psychological elements of spiritual warfare as part of his plea for us to walk in freedom:

"But now after you have known God, or rather are known by God, how is it that you turn again to the weak and beggarly elements, to which you desire again to be in bondage?" (Galatians 4:9).

The word *elements* here is a term for demonic lies. Demonic deception. The doctrines of demons and seducing spirits. Not just their teachings but even their presence. Paul is saying that some Christians actually turn away from God and back to actual demons, who may or may not be hiding behind fortune tellers, certain counselors, and even some church leaders.

These weak and beggarly demonic attacks make such a twist in your gut that you actually *desire again to be in bondage*. Let that sink in. Those are the words of Scripture—an actual desire for bondage.

You actually long for some kind of addiction, some kind of dysfunction, some kind of brokenness, some kind of devilish domination to suck all the dominion right out your fractured, messed up soul.

Dear friend, the Word of God understands you. The Word of God makes sense of you. This is broken psychology, and it is the devil's fiercest war.

It is also the devil's biggest area of victory: "For you did not receive the spirit of bondage again to fear, but you received the Spirit of adoption by whom we cry out, 'Abba, Father'" (Romans 8:15).

The Spirit of Adoption is a reference to the Holy Spirit. The Holy Spirit takes all the blessings that God has poured out on Jesus Christ, and makes them real in the life of every believer. One of these blessings is being adopted into God's family forever, so that you can cry out Abba, Daddy, Father. That is the Spirit whom God has given you.

But there is another spirit in this verse, and it doesn't come from God.

You did not receive the spirit of bondage again. Look at that word *again*. Salvation delivers you from every evil spirit. But as long as you are in this world, the devil will keep pulling you back. Don't go back to him *again*, because one of his greatest weapons is bondage, which is addiction, and one of his greatest bondages is *fear*.

If you are living in fear, if your soul is stuck on the fear setting, that is not the Spirit of God.

This is how spiritual warfare works. The devil focuses with laser beam precision on damaging your emotional health.

Your Heavenly Father focuses with far greater precision on making you whole:

> "The Spirit of the Lord is upon me, because he has anointed me to preach the gospel to the poor; he has sent me to heal the brokenhearted, to proclaim liberty to the captives and recovery of sight to the blind, to set at liberty those who are oppressed…" (Luke 4:18)

If you put everything in that verse together, you come up with two big truths that have been the foundation of this book, and of my lifetime of preaching and teaching as a pastor.

3. THE NEED: Eternal salvation is the indispensable foundation for deep emotional healing and psychological freedom.

There are a lot of ways to approach emotional healing. Counselors. Therapists. Medical interventions. Diet, sleep, nutrition.

I believe in all of the above.

But above all of them, I believe that the deepest emotional wholeness is only available to people who are saved. In fact, the biblical word for salvation, and the biblical word for healing are interchangeable, the noun *soteria* (so-tay-REE-uh) and the verb *sozo*.

Sin is the most emotionally damaging force in the universe. It is the mother of all dysfunction and the source of all addiction. It is the nucleus of depression and of despair. Sin breaks hearts, fractures relationships, and shatters hopes and dreams.

There is no solution to sin but the finished work of Jesus Christ on Calvary's Cross.

Calvary Love is the only antidote to sin. No therapist, medicine, healing arts, diet, nutrition, exercise, effort, performance, self-improvement, religion, and no *anything* can ever deliver even one soul from sin.

Only Jesus. Only the salvation he brings. There is no other way. There is no other hope. All emotional healing begins here, in salvation through His name: "Nor is there salvation in any other, for there is no other name under heaven given among men by which we must be saved" (Acts 4:12).

So if you are not saved, may I lovingly suggest you get saved today, and please quit putting that off.

4. GRACE: Grace comes to life at the intersection where theology meets psychology.

There are a lot of Christians with *very good theology* and *very messed up psychology*. Unless you let the love of Christ flood your soul—into every part of it—you will fall short of the grace of God again and again and again and again.

Here is Jesus Christ, the most wondrous and amazing person who has ever lived:

- He is fully God and fully human.
- He is the subject of every page of Scripture.
- Every prophet points to him.
- Every truth comes from him.
- Every prediction converges in him.
- The whole cosmos came from his creative hand.

- There is no one like him.
- There is no one beside him.
- He is the Messiah, the hope of the nations.
- Our Savior, Sanctifier, Healer, and Coming King.

The Person and Work of Christ is the most theologically rich and deep teaching in all of Scripture.

When Jesus begins his public ministry, he reads the Old Testament Scripture from Isaiah the prophet. That prophecy talks about the healing and deliverance of human psychology by means of eternal salvation.

He heals the brokenhearted. He proclaims liberty to the captives. He sets at liberty those who are oppressed. In other words:

As the theology of the Person and Work of Christ is increasingly applied to your soul, the power of grace brings about more and more emotional, psychological, sexual, physical, financial, and relational healing.

Jesus heals the broken-hearted.

How did he accomplish this?

Jesus shed his blood on the Cross, and died for your sins—those very sins which are the root of all human brokenness.

Then he rose again and ascended to heaven, all of which punched the devil in the head—hard enough to one day send him tumbling head over heels into the abyss of damnation forever.

This tells us that the great mission of Jesus is to liberate you from every dark force. That includes not only unburying you from the avalanche of sin, but shattering the prison bars of your bondage to Satan…

- So that you can be made whole.
- So that you can have an abundant life.

- So that you can walk in liberty.
- So that the joy of the Lord can be your strength.
- So that the Lord can be your ever present help in time of trouble.
- So that you can lie down beside still waters.
- So that you can say, He restores my soul.
- So that you can stand in victory.
- So that you can have hope.
- So that you can rise above your addictions.
- So that you can defeat your dysfunctions.
- So that you can know unfettered joy…

…all of which brings us to the pinnacle of Love-That-Never-Fails.

God cares about your emotional health.

Jesus cares about your emotional health.

So did the apostles.

So here comes the Apostle Paul. He sees the polluted, demonically defiled sea of insanity and immorality that we are all swimming in. He calls out its Big Lie.

5. THE WORLD: The philosophies of the world are so twisted by Satan they promise wholeness, but only deliver pain.

Paul urges and pleads and preaches and begs, *Oh, dear Christian, put on your breastplate! Guard your heart, because you will be eaten for lunch if you don't.*

I think the wonderful thing here is that the breastplate is very specific. It is the Breastplate of Righteousness. So let's turn our attention there.

THE BREASTPLATE OF RIGHTEOUSNESS

Paul picked the word righteousness because he knew it was the most important quality to fend off the devil's attack on your heart.

So let's start with this:

6. RIGHTEOUSNESS: Righteousness means goodness. Specifically, it means goodness that is good enough for God.

God is perfectly clear that none of us possesses this kind of goodness: "There is no one righteous, no not one" (Romans 3:10). "There is no one who does good, no not one" (Romans 3:12).

This means that no human being possesses the righteousness of God in and of themselves.

When you get saved, however, God does something wonderful.

God gives you his own righteousness: "I will greatly rejoice in the LORD, My soul shall be joyful in my God; For He has clothed me with the garments of salvation, He has covered me with the robe of righteousness, As a bridegroom decks himself with ornaments, And as a bride adorns herself with her jewels" (Isaiah 61:10).

Here is something God has *given*. Here is a gift from heaven to you. Here is something you receive the very moment that you are saved. Righteousness. The goodness of God. It is permanently and abundantly applied to your account.

Human righteousness cannot help you. Self-righteousness cannot help you. But God's righteousness is perfect. It is powerful. And, it is what you have been given, perfectly and without measure.

You, Christian, have "received the gift of righteousness" (Romans 5:17).

You didn't produce it; God freely gave it to you. This means that you are good enough for God because of God. This means you can live with nothing left to prove. This means that when God sees you, he sees you as being just like Christ, assuming you have been saved.

7. BREASTPLATE: The breastplate of righteousness refers to the righteousness purchased for us by Jesus at the Cross (2 Corinthians 5:21).

The biblical term for this is Justification. It is one of the greatest teachings in the Bible.

Justification captures in one word a profound and expansive theology. What Paul is saying here is that it is also a powerful and heart-protecting element of psychology too.

At salvation, a "breastplate" is issued to each new believer. It belongs to you all life long. The breastplate of righteousness has Christ's name stamped on it, as though He said, "Your righteousness isn't sufficient to protect you. Here, wear mine."

Now there is another kind of righteousness that comes to us from God. And that is a righteousness in how we live our lives. Wise choices. Holy living. Saying no to sin. Being kind and fair. Being loving to others. Generosity. Grace. That's righteousness too. But that kind of righteousness is called sanctification.

Justification is the righteousness God gives you as a free gift at the moment of salvation. This is the righteousness of your identity.

Sanctification is the holiness God works out in you as you walk with him and grow in grace by his Spirit. This is the righteousness of your behavior.

A lot of interpreters, when discussing the Breastplate of Righteousness, teach that this righteousness must be the righteousness of behavior. In fact, a large majority of Bible commentators take this position.

But I disagree, and I disagree strongly, and let me tell you why, and then you can make up your own mind—based on the Word of God.

The only way to live a righteous life is to wear the armor of

God. So how can you tell me that living a righteous life is one of the pieces of armor I have to wear to live a righteous life?

What?

Huh?

Are you really going to tell me that in order to live a righteous life I have to wear the armor of "living a righteous life"?

Do you get what I'm saying? The argument is completely circular.

If the breastplate of righteousness means the righteousness of *behavior*, then how can you put on the breastplate of righteousness, as a piece of armor that is essential in order to grow into righteousness of *behavior*? How is that supposed to happen?

I don't buy it. More on this in the next chapter. Then you can make up your own mind.

I'll just say how it works for me. Remember, this is spiritual warfare. Remember, the demons are real, they are vicious, and they are relentless. Remember we are talking about the piece of armor dedicated to emotional wholeness. And remember that the devil constantly attacks your psychology.

So here's how this works for me. I have had a lifelong struggle with a sense of unworthiness. It's one of the reasons I never wanted to be a pastor in the first place. It's one of the reasons I went for many years hoping that people didn't find out I actually had become a pastor. I just don't feel worthy.

My little church where I grew up was a travel agency for guilt trips.

So here's how the breastplate of righteousness works for me, when the devil tries to pierce my heart.

- The Devil says, You're a loser. I say no way! I am good enough for God. You're the loser.
- The Devil says, You're such a sinner. I say no way! God calls me a saint. I may have just sinned, but God still calls me a saint. Back off you ugly beast.

- The devil calls me condemned. I shout back, Justified.
- The devil calls me guilty. I shout back, Forgiven!
- The devil calls me weak and frail. I shout back, I am strong in the Lord and in the power of his might.
- The devil calls me rejected. I shout back, Accepted in the Beloved.
- The devil says I'm unworthy. But I say back, I've got the righteousness of Christ, and he is more than worthy enough for me.
- The devil accuses me night and day: you're blameworthy, dirty, and evil. But I wear the breastplate of righteousness to say: How can I be those things when God calls me blameless, and washed, and holy in his sight?
- The devil says, here's a temptation you just can't resist. But I say, Poor Devil, here's a breastplate you just can't overcome.

"Therefore take up the whole armor of God, that you may be able to withstand in the evil day, and having done all, to stand." (Ephesians 6:13)

If you would only grow and know your righteous standing in Christ, and if you would only protect your heart, and find your wholeness in him, then, when the evil day comes, and the depressing day comes, and the discouraging day comes, and the defeating day comes, and the pressure-filled day comes, and the tearful day comes, and the frustrating day comes, and the painful day comes, and the wounding day comes, and the cruel day comes, and the embarrassing day comes, and the shameful day comes, and the devastating day comes, and the dying day comes—and any day comes—you can stand in the evil day, and having done all, stand.

REFLECTION AND DISCUSSION

1. What do you think about the idea that the Bible has a lot to say about human psychology?
2. Describe some connections you see between broken psychology and spiritual warfare.
3. "Grace comes to life at the intersection where theology meets psychology." How do you react to this idea?
4. List some blessings and benefits from having been given the righteousness of God.
5. How could Romans 5:1 help strengthen you psychologically against Satan's attacks?

CHAPTER 8
THE BREASTPLATE OF RIGHTEOUSNESS, PART 2

Castle thyself within the power and promise of God for thy assistance and protection.
~William Gurnall

DAVID AND SAUL'S ARMOR

"Then David said to Saul, 'Let no man's heart fail because of him; your servant will go and fight with this Philistine.' And Saul said to David, 'You are not able to go against this Philistine to fight with him; for you are a youth, and he a man of war from his youth.'" (1 Samuel 17:32-33)

You probably know at least a little about David and Goliath. You might know that David, the young shepherd, defeated Goliath, the warrior-giant, with a slingshot and five smooth stones.

What you might not know is that before David went out to battle Goliath, he met with King Saul. David was a shepherd and he didn't have armor. So King Saul, who was a coward, offered his armor to David. As part of that conversation, he made his opinion of David's chances clear. "You are not able… to fight with him…" Nice pep talk, King.

David basically said, "Look, I'm a shepherd. I've fought mountain lions. I've fought bears. And besides, it's not me who has to fight the giant, it's God, so don't worry."

King Saul basically said, "David, you're nuts, But if you want to try, here, wear my armor."

> "So Saul clothed David with his armor, and he put a bronze helmet on his head; he also clothed him with a coat of mail. David fastened his sword to his armor…" (1 Samuel 17:38-39a)

Over there, taunting, mocking, insulting, hurting, is Goliath. He is an ambassador of demons. He is a servant of Satan, and an envoy of hell.

Let's let Goliath represent every giant you face. Goliath is every attack from the dark side. Goliath is the thing that makes you afraid, the worries that assail you, the addictions that control you, the dysfunctions that defeat you, the doctrines of demons and the flood of fictions sent from hell to devour you.

There's Goliath over there.

Over here is the little shepherd nobody believes in.

Whatever can you do?

Your friends, your family, your logic, and your culture all say, "You're doomed, but here, wear Saul's armor." Use human means to fight demonic battles. Use human effort to conquer spiritual problems.

Use the flesh to battle the flesh.

This is exactly the temptation we must resist if we are going to live in the Triumph of Grace. *The greatest temptation in spiritual warfare is to use* natural *weapons to fight battles only* supernatural *weapons can win.*

David refused Saul's armor and went forward with faith in God and not much else.

THE BREASTPLATE OF RIGHTEOUSNESS

The breastplate covered the heart and all the organs in the thoracic cavity, front and back.

Paul talks about it, because your psychological health sits in the crosshairs of the devil's attack. He wants to make you depressed, discouraged, dysfunctional, defeated, and if he can do it, dead by your own hand.

Peter's warning is not a joke: "Be sober, be vigilant; because your adversary the devil walks about like a roaring lion, seeking whom he may devour" (1 Peter 5:8).

What exactly is he devouring? What is the devil eating for lunch?

Not your body, but your soul. He's devouring your life. Your happiness. Your joy. Your love. Your sense of identity, your sense of agency. He's eating your dominion. Your purpose. Your mission.

All those things that have to do with psychological/emotional wholeness, happiness, and health. As we have seen, that is precisely what the breastplate protects.

I'd like to dig deeper into a truth we covered in the last chapter. It's important that we really understand this truth if we want to stand in victory.

I AM THE RIGHTEOUSNESS OF GOD IN CHRIST

> "For God made Him who knew no sin to be sin for us, that we might become the righteousness of God in Him." (2 Corinthians 5:21)

The invincible protection that stands between the devil's attack and your psychological health is your faith to wear the breastplate of righteousness.

Let's dig into that.

The invincible guardian that stands between the devil's attack and your psychological health is your tenacity to stand in the righteousness of Christ.

Here is one of the most soul-soothing promises in Scripture, from a prophet thousands of years ago.

> "For the mountains shall depart And the hills be removed, But My kindness [hesed = grace] shall not depart from you, Nor shall My covenant of peace be removed," Says the LORD, who has mercy [racham = emotional tenderness] on you. "O you afflicted one, Tossed with tempest, and not comforted, Behold, I will lay your stones with colorful gems, And lay your foundations with sapphires." (Isaiah 54:10-11)

The prophet is speaking to hurting, scared people, to people who have given up hope. The message he brings is both theological and psychological at the same time.

It is a theology of God who is full of grace and tender mercies.

It is a psychology of a life so good it is built on a foundation of and protected by walls made of sapphires and gems, meaning beauty and abundance.

Then Isaiah gives us the Old Testament corollary of Paul's New Testament shield of faith.

> "In righteousness you shall be established; You shall be far from oppression, for you shall not fear; And from terror, for it shall not come near you." (Isaiah 54:14)

In righteousness you shall be established. We can substitute the word *stabilized*. Wouldn't you like to be stabilized? If so, then righteousness is the key.

That would be the gift of God's righteousness, not your righteous living. I'll prove it below.

Think of your walk with the Lord. Ask yourself, Are you established in this truth of righteousness? Life can be destabilized, and life can be stabilized.

Do you believe in the righteousness of God in Christ, credited and counted and imputed to you once for all when you were saved?

Have you been made "the righteousness of God in Christ" or not?

Because if you take your stand on that truth, God promises you shall be far from oppression, and you shall not fear.

- Far from demonic oppression.
- Far from emotional oppression.
- Far from financial oppression.
- Far from political oppression.
- Far from physical oppression.

There will be something in your soul that cancels these things. Something that nullifies the bullies and fires a lethal stone into the forehead of your giants.

You shall be far from terror for it shall not come near you.

God says when you are established in righteousness, you will be far from oppression for you shall not fear; and from terror, for it shall not come near you.

The more you can say, "I am the righteousness of God in Christ" the more these promises come true.

- When you face an obstacle, declare "I am the righteousness of God in Christ."

- When you meet a giant, declare "I am the righteousness of God in Christ."
- When you confront a lie, declare "I am the righteousness of God in Christ."
- When you defy a dysfunction, attack an addiction, dislodge a demon, flatten a mountain, defeat your despair, declare, "I am the righteousness of God in Christ."

To stand in the gift of Christ's righteousness is to stabilize your soul and to protect your heart.

But you say, I'm not righteous. I keep doing bad stuff. I'm unlucky. I'm not worthy. I'm defeated. I'm stuck.

Echoing Satan's lies will never help you. You need new scripts and a new outlook. You need new habits. New patterns. New self-talk based on Scripture, not the devil's lie.

But when you simply say, "I am the righteousness of God in Christ," Jesus is glorified, and your whole psychology is made whole.

> "'No weapon formed against you shall prosper, And every tongue which rises against you in judgment You shall condemn. This is the heritage of the servants of the LORD, And their righteousness is from Me,' Says the LORD." (Isaiah 54:17)

This fallen world is a morally broken pain machine. Weapons will be formed by the enemy of your soul against you. Attacks will be launched against you.

- They will come from the lips of unwitting friends.
- They will come from the lips of enemies.
- They will come from comments on social media.
- They will come from the songs you hear.
- They will come from teachers and professors.

- They will come from news and so-called "objective sources."
- They will come from the left, from the right, and from below.

Weapons will be formed against you.

But no weapon formed against you shall prosper. Every tongue which rises against you in judgment, you shall condemn. This is the heritage of the servants of the Lord.

And do not miss that next line in this Scripture: "And their righteousness is from me, says the Lord." There it is. Not my righteousness but his. Not I but Christ.

Do you see this? Do you believe it?

Today, we are not condemned. We stand in the unclouded favor of Christ, because of his blood. We stand justified because of his sacrifice. And we stand vindicated, not in spite of his holiness, but because of his holiness.

You are to be emotionally stabilized and strengthened in the righteousness of God.

When you stand in the righteousness of Christ, no weapon formed against you shall prosper.

So let's pray:

> *O God I am not strong enough, not smart enough, and not good enough in myself to face this battle.*
> *But I take refuge in the shadow of your wing.*
> *And I stand clothed in the robe of your perfect righteousness.*
> *Therefore I step into this upcoming difficulty with the battle cry of victory on my lips.*
> *And I stand, tall and strong, in the victory of Christ... because I stand confident and secure in the righteousness of Christ.*

> *So I declare that no weapon formed against me shall prosper.*
> *And I say that every tongue which raises itself against me in judgment, I hereby condemn.*

God says, "your righteousness is from me." That is what you are established in. And the more you are established in it, the more these promises come true in your life.

I have had many critics through the years. And I'm not going to lie, it hurts and it undercuts my confidence too many times. My insecurities rise up and my heart sinks. It's easy to get discouraged. So I have to come back to this again and again.

I have to say, *I am the righteousness of God in Christ.*

He will vindicate me. He will come against my enemies. He will make their swords shatter, and the missiles go astray. He will frustrate their aims, and prevail over their plans.

So I want to give you five words to say, five words to mutter, five words to literally come out of your mouth, every single time the devil attacks your soul.

I mean when you feel like you're losing your mind, or you're under attack. You have to change what comes out of your mouth. You have to make what the Bible calls "a good confession" (1 Timothy 6:12).

DAVID AND SAUL'S ARMOR

There is young David, standing before King Saul. Over there is the wicked Giant Goliath, sent from the pit of hell to humiliate him.

> "So Saul clothed David with his armor, and he put a bronze helmet on his head; he also clothed him with a coat of mail. David fastened his sword to his armor and tried to walk, for he had not tested them. And David said to Saul, 'I cannot walk with these, for

I have not tested them.' So David took them off." (1 Samuel 17:38-39)

David took them off. I pray that you learn this lesson and keep coming back to it.

The more relentless the supernatural attack, the more useless the natural armor.

David took off Saul's armor. It didn't fit. It wouldn't work. He couldn't move. He couldn't breath. It wasn't for him.

We are talking about the divine breastplate of righteousness, not the breastplate of coping mechanisms you've developed.

Sooner or later, you need to take off the armor that you've invented to shield you from harm and trade it in for God's armor.

- You need to take off running away from problems.
- You need to take off glossing over spiritual problems with material success.
- You need to take off the armor of being the class clown.
- You need to take off the mask that you don't care—that you're indifferent—when you do care, and your pain runs deep.
- You need to take off drugs, and alcohol, and sexual sin; they're just numbing the pain of a wounded heart, but never healing the wound.
- You need to take off your mask of denial.
- You need to take off the self-talk that keeps you locked in despair: "I'm unlucky. I'm not good enough. God is against me. I'm a failure. I am cursed. I am not worthy of love. I am too different, too weird, too messed up for anyone to care. I am damaged goods. I look wrong, sound wrong, walk wrong, think wrong."

Put a guard on your lips, and say something else. Say five words to the problem. Say them to the mountain. Say them to the giant. Say them to the enemy. Say them to the demons and to the devil. But more important than all, say them to yourself.

> "Then David said to the Philistine, 'You come to me with a sword, with a spear, and with a javelin. But I come to you in the name of the LORD of hosts, the God of the armies of Israel, whom you have defied. This day the LORD will deliver you into my hand, and I will strike you and take your head from you. And this day I will give the carcasses of the camp of the Philistines to the birds of the air and the wild beasts of the earth, that all the earth may know that there is a God in Israel. Then all this assembly shall know that the LORD does not save with sword and spear; for... (1 Samuel 17:45-47)

Oh, my dear, hunted, haunted, wounded friend. Confused. Sad. Angry. Bitter. Unwanted or unloved. Ashamed. Bitter. Or just done.

You carry a load no human can bear. You fight a fight no human can win.

But the Lord does not save with a sword and spear or with any human device.

Here are five words to set you free.

Five words to immediately put on the breastplate of righteousness and to make God your stronghold in even the saddest struggle.

David declared them: Then all this assembly shall know that the LORD does not save with sword and spear; for THE BATTLE IS THE LORD's" (1 Samuel 17:47).

The battle is the Lord's.

Say it. Mutter it. Pray it. Declare it. Believe it.

The Battle is the Lord's.

- You can't run away from it, but the battle is the Lord's.
- You have to step into it, but the battle is the Lord's.

- You trust Christ in you to live through you in it, declaring the battle is the Lord's.
- You keep the faith, because the battle is the Lord's.
- You still show honor and respect, because the battle is the Lord's.
- You take a risk, step out in faith, because the battle is the Lord's.
- You guard your tongue, because the battle is the Lord's.
- You override fear with courage, because the battle is the Lord's.
- You step into the room, engage the awkward conversation, swallow your pride and ask for the date, send in the application, have the confrontation, deliver the apology and say an overdue I'm sorry—you someway, somehow step into the Great Unknown, onto the battlefield of the devil's world, and you live boldly…

Because the Battle is the Lord's!
Your job is faith. God's job is outcomes.

It doesn't matter if you look dumb. It doesn't matter even the outcomes. It doesn't even matter if you, in the natural, fail. Because in the spiritual, you are a champion, you are glorious, you are more than a conqueror, and for one shining moment, you have dominion, so the angels are applauding, the demons are fleeing, the devil is pouting, your God is smiling, your heart is strengthening, your psychology is healing, your burden is lightening, your muscles are growing, your maturity is deepening, your world is transforming, and eternal treasures beyond imagination are being stored up for you—heaps and heaps of them that will make the battle worth it all

Oh, Jesus, the all conquering King, before me, behind me, above me, below me, all around me, and in me—the battle is the Lord's.

What matters is that you overcame all that emotional resistance inside of you and for the first time, maybe in a long time, you did what God was calling you to do, saying as you did it, THE BATTLE IS THE LORD'S.

When you believe that, there is no such thing as failure.

REFLECTION AND DISCUSSION

1. What could be modern day equivalents of Saul's armor in your life? What quick fixes, unbiblical solutions, or even ungodly shortcuts might you be tempted to use in place of God's solutions?
2. What would it look like for you to take your stand in the righteousness of Christ? What would it sound like?
3. What kinds of oppression are you facing right now in your own spiritual warfare? What kind of attitudes are you displaying? How might you stand more fully on your righteousness in Christ?
4. What battles in your life—spiritual, moral, financial, relational, anything—do you need to turn over to the Lord?
5. According to 1 Corinthians 15:34, what is the result of embracing your righteous identity in Christ?

CHAPTER 9
THE BOOTS OF THE GOSPEL

The gospel, what is it but God's heart in print?
~William Gurnall

WEAR YOUR BOOTS

"Stand firm... having shod your feet with the preparation of the gospel of peace." (Ephesians 6:15)

Grammatically speaking, this is considered the most complicated piece of armor to decode. Paul could have simply said to put on your boots of the gospel. Instead he said to put on the boots which are the preparation of the gospel of peace.

Paul writes, "the preparation of the gospel of peace." He writes the word "of" twice. The preparation *of*... gospel *of*... In Greek grammar, this kind of phrase is called a genitive, and there are a lot of ways the genitive is used. In English, the most common way of translating a genitive is using the word *of*: the love of God, the way of salvation, the hope of eternal life, the home of Peter, the city of Ephesus. This is where Bible interpretation becomes so incredibly rewarding and fun.

A genitive construction simply takes two nouns (things), and says there is a relationship between them. In English, we indicate this by the order of words, and especially by using the word *of*. But Greek writers indicated this by slight changes in the spelling of each word to make it crystal clear that these two nouns are connected in a genitive relationship. Noun A relates to noun B. Now it is up to the context to determine the logical nature of that relationship. This is the job of the interpreter, in this case, us. We interpret Scripture the best we can.

Think deeply about those genitive phrases I just listed and ask yourself about the logic implied there. If you are a natural English speaker, you do this mental work in a split second, because you pick up the logic automatically, almost always.

But most of us are not natural Greek speakers, so we have to do some work.

For example, we have two nouns: city and Ephesus. When we join them in a genitive construction, we say "the city of Ephesus." What does "of" mean in that sentence? It means "which is." The city which is Ephesus. A is B. This is called a Genitive of Apposition.

We have the nouns home and Peter in a genitive relationship. This is most logically a Genitive of Possession, Peter's home.

What about "the love of God"? There are a couple of different and legit ways to go with this one. It can be a Genitive of Possession: the love which belongs to God, God's love. It is more likely to be a Genitive of Source: the love which comes from the source of God. I think that's the best option.

All genitives look the same grammatically, so it's the *interpreter* who has to decode which kind of genitive the original author of Scripture most likely meant. It's almost always clear. Sometimes, it might be up for debate; but this never actually affects any major areas of doctrine.

This is how biblical interpretation goes. We look carefully at the grammar, because the grammar is the Spirit-inspired means of conveying the truth and logic of God's Word.

Let's bring this back to the armor of God. In *the preparation of the gospel of peace*, we have two genitives. (There's another genitive lesson coming later in this book; please contain your enthusiasm.)

- The first *of* is a "Genitive of Source:" the preparation that comes from the source of the gospel.
- The second *of* is a "Genitive of Substance:" the gospel which is, in essence, a message of peace.

Note: this is my interpretation of these genitives. Other interpreters might disagree, but then it is their job to write a book and make their case and then get you to read it! End of the grammar lesson; good job. Paul is saying that this piece of armor bolts together 3 theological parts:

1. Preparation… which comes from…
2. The Gospel… which is a message of…
3. Peace… between God and believers.

Let's take those one at a time, and then put them together.

PREPARATION

The Greek word, which is *hetoimasia* [het-toy-mah-SEE-uh], and the idea can be interpreted in one of two ways.

Under the first way, the idea is that you should be sharing the gospel, sharing Christ, out there evangelizing, and joining a church that gets a lot of people saved.

All of that is true, important, and good. If you know me, I love this. I'm all about evangelism, and I'm all about putting God's people on an evangelistic footing. It's not happening in American churches like it should be happening. We need to get more people saved.

However that's not what this first genitive, "the preparation of the gospel," is primarily about. The preparation of the gospel is not mainly about evangelizing lost people; it's much more about equipping saved people so they know the gospel and stand firmly in it when the devil smacks them with doubt. I want to make that my first main lesson in this chapter.

1. The preparation of the gospel is mainly about equipping saved people to stand so strongly on the gospel that the devil can't slip in a guilt trip edgewise.

It's not so much the preparation that comes *for* preaching gospel; it's mainly the preparation that comes *from you really embracing the gospel.* If you know the gospel inside and out, you are ready for the devil's attack. You have a readiness whatever this morally broken world throws at you.

- You are ready *mentally,* because you know the truths that set you free and keep you free and make you strong.
- You are ready *psychologically,* because the promises of God have seeped down from your mind into your emotions, bringing healing, and deliverance, and victory, and strength.
- You are ready *spiritually,* because grace puts muscle on your faith and courage in your heart so the devil can't mess with you.

The best preparation is to know the gospel inside and out. The heart of the gospel is the Cross of Christ. When you lean hard on Calvary Love, the devil cannot embarrass you with guilt. He cannot immobilize you with doubt. He cannot break you with shame. His accusations bounce off of your armor. Really knowing the gospel is the essential preparation for you to engage the great mission of Evangelism with gusto and grace.

This is not so much so that you can preach it; it is more so that you can rest in it, and find confidence, hope, and strength for yourself in the gospel.

Back in the days when David faced Goliath, David had a secret weapon, and it wasn't his slingshot or five smooth stones.

His secret weapon was that he had something in his soul that neither his brothers nor the other soldiers had. David stood before that giant, nine feet tall, and shouted, "Who is this uncircumcised Philistine that he should defy the armies of the living God?"

What did he have in his heart?

- He knew who he was: he was a solider in the armies of the living God by grace through faith.
- He knew who his enemy was: this uncircumcised Philistine, meaning a secular, morally corrupt opponent of God.
- He knew who God was: the living God. The one and only. The source of everything good, and especially of the gospel of grace.

David's secret weapon was the preparation of the gospel—that gospel energized him tremendously as a child of God.

2. The secret weapon of a victorious Christian is a mindset made ready for the fight by prolonged exposure to the gospel of the grace of God.

This is why David could face Goliath and the others couldn't. He wore footwear that none of the others did.

When demons seek to infiltrate your heart and life, it is your solid footing in the gospel of grace that will frustrate their plans and make them give up in defeat.

Here is a man caught up in a war with a monster, a giant, something too big to handle. And here we are. We're in the same battle against that same monster, that same giant. It's more than we can handle.

The devil hits you from every angle he can.

- He'll make you think everybody else thinks you're stupid.
- He'll remind you of past mistakes till you obsess over them.
- He'll discourage you with troubles and then lie that they're God's fault.
- He'll tempt you in areas he knows you're already weak, so here come food addictions, sex addictions, porn addictions, drug, alcohol, gambling, shopping addictions. The devil hits you where you're weak.
- He'll drive a wedge between you and your spouse.
- He'll convince you you're damaged goods.
- He'll roar like a lion, bellow like a giant, hiss like a serpent, or seduce like an angel.

When you climb up into your dignity and dominion, the devil will con your own team to pull you back down to their limp, wimpy, risk-averse safe zone. The devil hits you from every angle.

3. A Triumphant Spirit is unshakable faith built up by continually hearing and studying the love of God in the Grace of Christ.

You live in a world of troubles. The only way to "glory in tribulations" as the Bible says, is if the love of God has been poured out in your heart (Romans 5:5).

You need to hear about the love of God over and over again.

About the grace of God over and over again. About the Cross of Christ, over and over again. About the unsearchable riches of Christ over and over again.

We hear so much preaching and so much teaching about the duties and requirements and obligations of the faith. Do this, don't do that, and you'd better bear fruit!

We hear so much about signs and wonders and new revelations and encounters that we're tempted to chase experiences and measure faith by emotions.

But we hear so very little about Jesus and his blood-bought love. If your heart isn't rooted and grounded in the love of God, if your soul isn't stabilized by grace, if your mind isn't informed of the intricate interlocking truths of Christ in his Person and Calvary Love, if your troubled past isn't delivered and healed under grace, and if your dominion isn't fortified by a prolonged and continuous exposure to the magnificent edifice of truth called grace, then you become easy prey for Satan.

For every Goliath that comes your way, you'll be back there in the tents with David's scaredy-cat brothers, making excuses and blaming others and shivering with fright. Or you'll be over there with crazy King Saul, alternating between bullying and denial again and again.

When Paul said to put on "the preparation" he meant a *triumphant spirit*! He meant an energy, confidence, and calmness that can only come from one source.

THE GOSPEL

Gospel is a theological word with a rich and profound meaning. The Greek word is *evangelion* (the g is hard, ev-on-guh-LEE-on). Take the word for *good* and mash it into the word for *news*, and you get this word. Good News.

Satan hates the Gospel. He has done a fantastic job of distorting it — mainly among Christians. Especially among, and I hate to say it, pastors.

I think the most clarifying phrase for the Gospel comes from the lips of Paul speaking to pastors in Ephesus as he's on his way to death. Paul called it "the gospel of the grace of God" (Acts 20:24). If there is anything you should know about the Gospel it is that grace is its heart and soul.

So what is this Gospel of Grace?

1. The Gospel is the love of God reaching out to prodigals and forgiving them, washing them, blessing them (enriching them), and bringing them to heaven, all without the slightest compromise to God's own holiness.

Under the Gospel of grace the *love* of God is fulfilled, because the closest possible relationship of access and care is created between you and your Maker. Grace is the Love of God poured out on the one who believes the Gospel.

But also under grace—and this is the utterly exclusive message of biblical Christianity—the *holiness* of God is fulfilled because every moral failure is fully punished and completely cleansed by the sacrifice of Jesus on the Cross.

Grace is the kindness of God poured out on sinners-turned-into-saints *because of* the satisfaction of divine holiness at the Cross of Christ. In other words, there are five non-negotiable ingredients in the recipe of grace:

1. The love of God
2. The inflexible holiness of God
3. The sinfulness of humans
4. The complete helplessness of humans
5. The Cross of Christ

Skip even one of them and what you're left with is an ugly distortion of the biblical doctrine of grace.

Divine Holiness and Divine Love meet at the Cross. So Scripture declares that God is both *just* (that's his holiness) and the *justifier* of the one who has faith in Jesus (that's his grace) (Romans 3:26).

2. The Gospel is the work of God alone through the finished work of the Christ on the Cross.

There could be no Gospel apart from the death of Jesus and the blood he shed. Whatever had to happen to bring a sinner back to God — you, me, anybody — whatever had to happen actually did happen on the day Jesus died.

He suffered. He carried our sins. He absorbed all the punishment. Whatever condemnation our sins deserved, whatever, whatever justice, whatever anything, Jesus himself took into himself on the Cross and paid the price in full. So Paul exclaims, "God forbid that I should boast except in the Cross of Christ" (Galatians 6:14).

This Gospel of Grace is exclusive. There is nothing like it in all the annals of all of earth's long history. The Gospel excludes everything else. It wipes it all off the table. It's Jesus or it's nothing. In the gospel, Jesus and his finished work on Calvary, crowds out everything else. Only Jesus is left standing.

> ANY MESSAGE YOU HEAR THAT PUTS ANY FRACTION OF ANY BURDEN ON YOUR SHOULDERS FOR YOUR SALVATION IS NOT THE GOSPEL.

3. The Gospel is the gift of God and cannot coexist with any human effort whatsoever.

- No good works
- No morality
- No sacrifice
- No self-sacrifice
- No obedience
- No religion
- No ritual
- No mystical experience
- No effort
- No payment
- No improvement
- No performance
- No character
- No paying forward
- No giving back
- No human virtue
- No repentance
- No surrender
- No following
- No nothing

Not one speck of any human virtue can mix with the finished work of Jesus Christ.

To suggest that you can add even the tiniest droplet to what Jesus did on the Cross is to insult the Savior and to devalue the work of Christ.

No. The Gospel we preach is Christ alone. And the acid test of the validity of the Gospel is exactly this. *What does it make of Jesus Christ and him crucified? Is he part of it or is he all?*

We will declare till our dying breath, that Jesus Christ and him Crucified is all the gospel we need, now and forevermore.

4. The Gospel is the call of God to all the world to turn from

every other possible hope to *faith alone* in Christ alone to bring you back to God.

- For by grace you are saved through *faith*. (Ephesians 2:8)
- Therefore a person is justified by *faith* apart from the works of the law. (Romans 3:20).
- We have the righteousness which is from God by *faith*. (Philippians 3:9)

Faith is the only thing a human can *do* that isn't a work. No merit badge goes to faith, because faith pins the merit badge on the Person you're believing in.

Faith is not a work. Faith is an unwork.

This means that the Gospel is the Good News that you can end your striving, end your working, end your sweating and straining and worries and fear.

Trust in Jesus is all it takes. It's as easy as ABC.

1. ADMIT you need a Savior.
2. BELIEVE Jesus, the Crucified and Risen Savior, is the One.
3. CHOOSE to put your faith in him.

There are two errors that make my head explode when it comes to teaching and preaching the gospel.

The first error is when the message preached doesn't mention the Cross of Christ. *Without the death of Christ, you're not hearing the Gospel.* This is a fatal flaw.

The second error is when the message demands that the sinner carries even a fraction of the burden for their own salvation.

So many Christian cliches propagate this error.

- It's not the Gospel to *give your life to Christ*. The Gospel is that Christ gave his life for you. He's the giver; you're the receiver. All these cliches tragically turn the gospel on its head.

- It's not the Gospel to *surrender* your life to Christ. In the Gospel, he surrendered his life to the nails of Calvary's Cross.
- It's not the Gospel to *repent* and become a different person. That's a burden no one can bear. In the Gospel the only thing you repent of is the delusion you can make yourself a better person who is good enough for God.
- It's not the Gospel to *ask Jesus into your heart* unless that heart has been first made clean by believing in the Crucified and Risen Savior as your only hope. The problem with this cliche is that it bypasses Calvary altogether (plus, this language is not in the Bible).
- It's not the Gospel that you *give, do, perform, or follow* anyone, anywhere, anyhow. How is any of that good news? The Good News is that Jesus is following you with *his* goodness and mercy all the days of your life, and if you put your faith in him, you will dwell in the house of the Lord forever (Psalm 23:6). Only *after* you are saved are you capable of following him with your life.

It's faith, faith, faith, faith, faith. It's faith plus nothing, in the matchless Gospel of the Grace of God.

In every battle, with every giant, and in every demonic assault, you simply fall back into the arms of grace and see the salvation of the Lord.

Even when the giant hurled his insults at David, David shouted forth one of the greatest statements of grace in all of Scripture: "Then all this assembly shall know that the LORD does not save with sword and spear [human effort]; for the battle is the LORD's..." (1 Samuel 17:47).

The work is the Lord's. Salvation is the Lord's. Forgiveness is the Lord's. Your entry to heaven belongs to the Lord.

When Paul wanted to point to the *one thing* that would give your feet a firm footing, and prepare you to stand, to not lose it, and to not lose hope, he compared those boots to the precious gospel of the Grace of God. The preparation arises from the gospel alone.

But there's one more element to make your boots complete.

It's the *preparation of the gospel of peace.*

PEACE

If you could bottle peace and sell it, you'd be the richest person in history.

The word in Greek is *eirene* (eye-RAY-nay) and in Hebrew is *shalom*. It includes the absence of strife, but it means so much more. It's a really big word, and it includes wholeness, abundance, health, prosperity, joy, and happiness, and everything a person would ever want. This is the life. Peace is true life. Peace is real life.

It begins with peace with God. That's the first thing and the main thing.

The technical term for peace with God is *reconciliation*. This concept is taught in many places in Scripture.

Scripture is clear that in our fallen condition, we are actually at war with God, morally speaking: "And you, who once were alienated and enemies in your mind by wicked works, yet now He has reconciled" (Colossians 1:21).

There's no escaping the fact that the unsaved person is locked in the grip of the powers of darkness. Paul's analysis is devastating:

> "And you He made alive, who were dead in trespasses and sins, in which you once walked according to the course of this world, according to the prince of the power of the air, the spirit who now works in the sons of disobedience, among whom also we all once conducted ourselves in the lusts of our flesh, fulfilling the desires

of the flesh and of the mind, and were by nature children of wrath, just as the others." (Ephesians 2:1-3)

To be unsaved is to be on the wrong side of the war. It is to be under the influence of demons. It is to be gripped by devil's dark power (Colossians 1:13). The unsaved person is at war with God.

When we believe the Gospel, the war is over. This is the only way, and the only conceivable way, to find peace with God: "Therefore, having been justified by faith, we have peace with God through our Lord Jesus Christ," (Romans 5:1).

All peace starts here. There is an anxiety, and an unsettledness in the heart until you have made peace with God. This is why the unbelieving world is so chaotic. The whole world is easy prey for Satan, because the whole world is in rebellion against God.

As Christians, we are ambassadors for Christ to a world, a culture, and a friendship circle that is at war with God. Our central message is so simple, so clear, and so hated: "Be reconciled to God" (2 Corinthians 5:20).

1. The deepest peace starts with peace with God through saving faith in Christ.

Do you want stability in your life? Make peace with God. Because that is the start of a peaceful heart in the midst of all the battles of your life.

As I write this book, I am in my 45th year as a pastor. It shocks me that I'm still in this, mainly because I've never seen myself as worthy. But I know my worthiness is of the Lord. To God be the glory. He has qualified me (Colossians 1:12). I do believe I've got a lot more years in me. I don't feel even close to being done, Lord willing.

But, I've seen a few things over these years.

Working in church ministry concentrates a lot of both ugliness and beauty.

We hear all the good stuff in thousands of people's lives. All the engagements come to us. All the weddings. The much-wanted pregnancies and births. The answered prayers. The good news and healings. Days and years of sobriety. We hear that good news a lot.

But we also hear bad news a lot. We hear of so much chaos and struggle. We actually hear the bad stuff more. Pray for this sickness. For this shattered marriage. These messed up children. This evil boss. This demonic attack. We hear of Addictions. Infidelities. Struggles. We're told of so much sadness. So much depression. We hear too many times the ultimate heartbreak of those desperate souls who have ended their own lives at their own hands. The spiritual warfare of life is a very real thing to anyone who has been in ministry for a while.

Church life concentrates the bad stuff. I've been taking in these stories now for 45 years. As pastors, we want to hear those stories. We want to come alongside you. We want to bring grace and healing and peace to you by setting you on the truth.

But here is what I have seen over and over again:

2. The deepest peace in every category belongs those who are deeply rooted and grounded in the love of God and in his matchless grace.

True mental health, is set on the foundation of the Gospel of the grace of God, because it is the Gospel of Peace.

That is why in the spiritual battle of our lives, we have to strap on the readiness that comes from the Gospel of Peace.

> DEMONS CAN DO NOTHING TO YOU WHEN YOU HAVE ANCHORED YOUR SOUL IN THE TRIUMPH OF THE CRUCIFIED ONE.

Paul writes, "Stand firm... having shod your feet with the

preparation of the gospel of peace" (Ephesians 6:15). The difference between people who collapse and lose it, versus people who grieve and mourn and suffer with dignity and hope, is exactly this: *Believers who thrive are those who have a firm, unshakable footing in the Saving Work of Christ and in its powerful implications for every area of life.*

This attitude scares the devil. It frightens the demons away. Demons can do nothing to you when you have anchored your soul in the Triumph of the Crucified One.

Every time a giant comes, after the initial shock, you can reach into a grace that goes from the top of your head to the soles of your feet, and then say with certainty, *Who is this uncircumcised Philistine to defy a soldier of the living God? I will not fear, for The Battle Is the Lord's.*

REFLECTION AND DISCUSSION

1. How would you restate or summarize the grammatical information at the start of this chapter? How important is it to dig into biblical grammar?
2. What is your reaction to the critique of "Christian cliches" in this chapter? Have you heard the terms included in this list (give your life to Christ, surrender, repent, etc.)? In your opinion, how fair is this critique?
3. State the biblical concept of reconciliation in your own terms. Why do you think this is so central and so crucial?
4. "Demons can do nothing to you when you have anchored your soul in the triumph of Christ." Comment and react to this quote.
5. This question will require you to think really hard. What connections can you see between this chapter and Paul's

message in Romans 5:1-5? Hint: figure out from this Scripture how it is that a believer can "glory in tribulations."

CHAPTER 10
THE SHIELD OF FAITH

Armour is suitable for earth, but robes for heaven. Hope goes into the field and waits on the Christian till the last battle be fought and the field cleared, and then faith and hope together carry him in the chariot of the promise to heaven's door, where they deliver up his soul into the hands of love and joy, which stand ready to conduct him into the blissful presence of God.
~William Gurnall

THE FIERY SERPENTS

"Above all, taking the shield of faith with which you will be able to quench all the fiery darts of the wicked one." (Ephesians 6:16)

There's an amazing account in the Old Testament during the wilderness wanderings of the children of Israel. They are in the wilderness by their own choice, and they are, as usual, complaining. Complaining is always a mark that faith has evaporated.

They are bitter. They are angry. They are unfaithful. "So the LORD sent [unleashed] fiery serpents among the people, and they bit the people; and many of the people of Israel died." (Numbers 21:6)

So let me point out that the word that is translated "sent" doesn't exactly mean that. The Hebrew word is *shalach*. It means to set free, unleash, or to let go.

God had his hand of protection on the people. This was grace. He was holding back the evil, protecting them from danger, and blockading them from fiery serpents. But when they abused that grace again and again, he lifted his hand of protection and gave them what they asked for which was *a life without the intervention of God.*

Sometimes you get what you want and then don't want what you get.

Immediately the Giant Pain Machine of this fallen world had its unfettered way. In came fiery serpents.

So the people are sorry, of course, and they run to Moses. *Help us! Help us! Pray for us!*

Moses prayed for them, and God gave him some very strange instructions. "Make a bronze serpent, put it on a pole, and stand it up in he middle of the camp," said God. "Tell everyone who has been bitten by a serpent to come and look at the serpent, and they will live."

It's kind of ludicrous, don't you think? Can you imagine the conversations in all the tents? *What? Look at a bronze serpent and live? Look and live is crazy!*

That didn't stop Moses. "So Moses made a bronze serpent, and put it on a pole; and so it was, if a serpent had bitten anyone, when he looked at [unto] the bronze serpent, he lived." (Numbers 21:9)

Moses states a powerful truth here, but it's not brought out well in the English translation of the original Hebrew. He didn't write "when he looked *at* the serpent." Moses wrote, "when he looked *unto* the serpent." The only way you would drag your snake bitten self to look at that serpent was if you believed enough to look unto the serpent in faith. You either believed this would work (even a little) or not.

Looking "unto" something implies faith. Faith means trust. We have the same Hebrew phrase in Isaiah's prophecy: "Look to [unto] Me, and be saved, All you ends of the earth! For I am God, and there is no other." (Isaiah 45:22) Trust me. Believe in me and be saved.

Moses is saying that salvation from snake bites came to the one who believed enough to just look at the bronze snake lifted up for all to see.

Fifteen centuries later, Jesus told religious Nicodemus, "And as Moses lifted up the serpent in the wilderness, even so must the Son of Man be lifted up, that whoever believes in Him should not perish but have eternal life." (John 3:14-15)

Jesus essentially said "I am the bronze serpent..." *Bronze*, because bronze combines two metals, and Jesus combines two natures. *Serpent* because serpent indicates sin, and Jesus was made sin for us to die the death penalty we deserved (2 Corinthians 5:21). *Lifted up* because the bronze serpent was lifted up on a pole and Jesus was lifted up on a cross. And in both cases, one *look of faith* was all it took to be saved. Look and live, brother. Look and live sister. Look to Jesus Christ and live.

THE SHIELD

> "Above all, taking the shield of faith with which you will be able to quench all the fiery darts of the wicked one." (Ephesians 6:16)

This verse illustrates faith as a shield and illustrates satanic oppression as fiery darts.

Let's start with the shield. The Roman soldier was equipped with one of two shields. A small round one, and a big rectangular one. The small round shield was called a *buckler*, but that's not what Paul means here.

The word here means the big rectangular shield. The Greek word for this is *thureos*, which literally means *door*, because that's what this shield looked like. In fact, the ancient writer Homer explains that soldiers would use their shields as doors to block the entrance to the houses they were staying in during war.

The *thureos* was four feet high and two and a half feet wide. It was made of wood, and it was covered with leather. We'll come back to this leather in a minute. The shield had straps for the soldier to hold it.

Some shields also had hooks on the sides, on the top, and the bottom. A company of Roman shoulders could stand in rows. The first row could hook their shields together in front of them. This would make an impenetrable wall against arrows and spears. The back rows could lift their shields over their heads, and hook them together too. The whole company was like a giant turtle moving forward. All the arrows, spears, and rocks that rained down on them would just bounce off.

By naming this specific shield, you get the idea that this is a heavily armed soldier.

This shield is piece of armor number four. Armor pieces one, two, and three attach to your body. You wear them: the belt of truth, the breastplate of righteousness, the boots of the gospel of peace.

But this one, you don't wear, you carry. That's why the verse begins with the words, "Above all..." The shield covers the first three defenses. *Faith is a defense for your defenses.* Faith is your double protection in this great spiritual war.

THE FIERY DARTS

The shield of faith is God's supernatural resource for you to quench all the fiery darts of the devil.

Ancient warriors dipped the tips of their arrows in something sticky and flammable, like tar. They set it on fire and shot. So this is a double danger. If the tip doesn't penetrate you, you still have to deal with the fire. But have no fear, if you have this shield. Because the leather covering on the shield could withstand the fire, unlike the wood beneath it.

In this illustration, notice who's shooting the flaming arrows: these are the fiery darts of the Wicked One.

Do you realize that Satan himself is firing flaming arrows at you all the time?

Why does Scripture liken them to arrows? Because they come from a distance and they pierce.

Why flaming arrows? Because once they pierce, they spread. An arrow pierces which is bad enough, but a fire spreads, which makes it worse.

What are these flaming arrows? These flaming arrows represent every attack from the devil and his demons. Temptations, troubles, discouragements, doubts, fears, bitterness, and more. You name it. Anything that drives a wedge between you and God, between you and the people you love, or between you and your deepest identity in Christ, is a fiery dart of the devil.

It's important to realize that the devil not only works in overtly evil ways, he's also very sneaky. His attacks can be either overt or covert. Most of them are covert. Many of his fiery darts *feel* like warm hugs. He disguises his attacks. Never forget that he is, above all else, subtle. For example, you might feel that it is a loving thing to actually affirm someone else in their sins. Jesus was a friend of sinners, right?

Right. But he never affirmed people's sins; he delivered them from their sins. He showed them the way out of Satan's trap. When you actually affirm someone in their sins, and feel good about doing that, it means there's an arrow sticking out of your back flaming with fire.

The fiery darts of the evil one come in all shapes and sizes.

The only way to extinguish them is faith. So what is that? How does faith quench these attacks of Satan? We really need to understand the word *faith*. It's the one thing that shields you from Satan's fiery darts. In a sense, faith is the one thing that makes all the other things easy.

So let's dig deep. Hang on.

THE ANATOMY OF FAITH

1. Faith has a subject and an object.

When scholars analyze faith, they divide it into two main parts:

- The subject of faith — That's the person doing the believing.
- The object part — That's the thing or person that's actually believed.

So, let's take the simple sentence: *I believe in Jesus.* In this sentence, the subject of faith is I and the object of faith is Jesus.

So faith means someone believing *in* someone or something. The one who believes is the subject of faith. The something that is believed is called the object of faith. Got it?

This subject/object structure is clear throughout Scripture. For example, Paul writes:

> "[K]nowing that a man is not justified by the works of the law but by faith in Jesus Christ, even we have believed in Christ Jesus, that we might be justified by faith in Christ and not by the works of the law; for by the works of the law no flesh shall be justified." (Galatians 2:16)

This is extremely important because Satan has worked out a

whole lot of strategies against faith by confusing the subject and object.

One of his most successful strategies is to substitute anything but Christ-Crucified as the object of faith. *It's doesn't matter who you believe, just believe in something,* he says. For religious/legalistic people, it's good works. For secular people, it's the glories of human nature. For confused Christians, it's "the kingdom," a nebulous phrase at best.

Another strategy is to mix two objects together. A little bit of this and a little bit of that. A little bit of good works and a little bit of Jesus. A little bit of morality and a little bit of church. I'll believe in Jesus on Sundays and Mammon on Mondays and Horoscopes on Tuesdays. We can blend Christ and works, Grace and Law, the Gospel and human performance. The truth is that to mix together Christ plus *anything* is to shatter faith into a million tiny pieces.

Another satanic strategy is to make you the object of your own faith. I believe in me, myself, and I.

Yet another really big strategy is to remove the object altogether. Just believe. Just have faith. Believe in what? Nobody. Just believe.

One more satanic strategy is to say that only subjects who are "predestined" by God can have faith. The theology is often called hyper-Calvinism, which suggests that God has pre-selected which individuals can and can't be saved; if you're not predestined, tough luck, no salvation for you. Wrong and no. Faith is universal. Everyone has faith, not just the so-called "predestined."

In reality, when people do not have faith in Christ, the problem isn't the subject—that they're not "predestinated" so they have no faith. No. They have plenty of faith. *Everybody* does. Everybody has faith in something. The problem isn't an inability to have faith—a problem with the *subject* of faith. The problem is lots of faith in the wrong *object*. They're believing just fine. Unfortunately, they are believing in anyone and anything except Jesus the Savior.

All of this confusion is satanic. All of this is part of our battle.

When those fiery serpents bit the people, and Moses said Look and live... who was the subject? The snake-bitten person. Who was the object? The serpent lifted on the pole. Put your faith there and live.

So far so good?

2. Faith is only as good as its object.

So let's take this sentence: *John believes in the Tooth Fairy.* The subject is... John. The object is... the Tooth Fairy.

How strong, how reliable, how real is the object? Not so much. What if it's faith in Santa Claus? What if it's faith in Zeus or Zoroaster or the million gods of Hinduism? Or faith in Atheism? Or faith in horoscopes and fortune tellers?

Faith is only as good as its object.

The devil attacks this too. He says, *Just believe.* You say, *Believe in what?* The devil says, *Anything. It doesn't matter.*

But it does matter because if the object of faith is unreal, unreliable, non-sensical, or absurd, you can believe with all your might and it still won't do you any good. As the Psalmist said, "Some trust in chariots, and some in horses; But we will remember the name of the LORD our God" (Psalm 20:7).

3. It's not the sincerity of the subject, it's the reliability of the object that matters most.

So when those snakes bit the people, and they were called to trust in the uplifted bronze serpent, only one thing mattered: *Was that object of faith sufficient to save them or not?*

When it comes to eternal salvation from sin, we have the same question. *Is Jesus Christ, crucified and risen again, a sufficient object of faith to save us from our sins?* Scripture answers with a resounding YES echoing down the corridors of forever.

Jesus says, *Come to Me. I am enough. I am all you need. I am all you will ever need. My death on the cross for you is not only sufficient, but all-*

sufficient and hyper-sufficient. My Calvary Love is more than enough to remove the venom of sin. More than enough to give you eternal life. Look and live. Look unto me and be saved.

If Jesus Christ is the object of your faith, then your faith is as real and as strong as Jesus Christ himself.

Now, let's go next level.

4. Faith is non-meritorious.

We believe in non-meritorious saving faith. Nobody gets a merit badge for believing in someone else. There is no virtue in the act of faith itself (the subject of faith). All the virtue, and all the merit, lies in the object of faith.

> THERE'S NO VIRTUE OR MERIT IN THE SUBJECT. ALL THE VIRTUE AND MERIT IS IN THE OBJECT (JESUS).

For example, I believe in the chair I'm sitting in as I write this. When I stand beside the chair, I'm working, and the chair is not working. But when I believe in the chair, and sit down in it, I stop working, and the chair starts working. In fact, sitting in the chair is awesome. I'm am no longer holding up my weight, the chair is holding my weight. If you want to give a merit badge for somebody doing a good job, you give it to the chair. The moment I sit down, I shift from working to resting.

I hope you're getting this, because there's a really important statement in theology.

Faith is non-meritorious.

So what? Here's the so what. When you understand that faith is non-meritorious, you protect grace. Faith is not a good work. Faith is not an effort. Faith is the cessation of effort. It's not a work, it's an unwork.

FAITH IS AN UNWORK.

The subject of faith never gets a pat on the back for faith. The pat on the back goes to the object of faith, to Jesus. *He* saved you. Faith did not save you, Jesus did. Faith did not die on the Cross for your sins. Jesus did. Faith did not shed any blood, pay any price, earn any praise. All of that was accomplished by our crucified Savior.

He gets all the glory. He gets all the honor. He possesses all the merit. He alone is to be praised. We've got nothing to boast about (Ephesians 2:8,9), because we did nothing to save ourselves but to *stop working*. That's why we maintain that faith is non-meritorious. Get it?

So the conniving devil attacks this. He works overtime to make faith itself meritorious. Oh, he says, have faith in faith because faith is all you need, and it's all you need because faith has merit.

Lie!

To say that the subject of faith has merit is to murder grace. It is to make faith a good work and to pin a merit badge on the one who believes rather than the One who died. In truth, faith is a little tiny zero resting its weight on a great big infinity of Calvary Love. So Paul declares, "Therefore it is of faith that it might be according to grace…" (Romans 4:16). The subject of faith isn't good; the object of faith is good, and that's why human faith and divine grace mesh together so perfectly.

I told you we were going deep. But there's more.

5. Saving faith is exclusive.

Being saved means having one and only one object of faith: Jesus Christ, who died for your sins and rose again.

It's not "Jesus-plus."

It's not "Jesus-and."

It's just Jesus.

Eternal Salvation excludes every other hope from the object of faith. If you're believing in Jesus plus your baptism, you're not saved. If you're believing in Jesus plus your morality, you're not saved. If you're believing in Jesus plus your religion, good works, or Buddha, you're not saved. "Jesus said to him, 'I am the way, the truth, and the life. No one comes to the Father except through Me'" (John 14:6).

That's as exclusive as it gets.

So, here's a definition of saving faith:

6. SAVING FAITH means claiming by personal choice, and relying exclusively upon the finished work of Jesus Christ on the cross as my only hope for salvation.

The finished work of Christ is everything. We don't talk about it enough. In his dying breaths, Jesus cried out one word: FINISHED! (John 19:30)

That means that his death was the only death needed. His condemnation, his damnation, his punishment, his suffering, his receiving our sins and shame, his guilt, his everything is all that is needed.

Faith in the finished work of Christ is saving faith.

> *Lifted up was he to die,*
> *IT IS FINISHED was his cry,*
> *Now in heaven, exalted high!*
> *Hallelujah! What a Savior!*

You can't look two ways. You can't be double-minded here. You're looking to Christ, or to something else. There is no other antidote to the venom of sin. No salvation anywhere but him.

So, the one and only efficacious object of faith in the Christian life is Jesus Christ and his finished work on our behalf. Christians declare "faith alone in Christ alone."

This is faith. There is nothing complex about the subject and everything complex about the object, because the object has to be sufficient and efficacious, and if you have Jesus, he is.

So, now we have learned a bit about faith. When Paul urges you to cover your life with the shield of faith, what exactly does that mean? Let's go back to where we started.

THE SHIELD OF FAITH

So, whether you have fiery darts coming at you, which is Satan's fault, or fiery serpents, which is your own fault, the solution is the same: The Shield of Faith.

Actually, it's *faith*. The shield is just an illustration. Don't focus on it. Focus on faith. The shield which is faith (genitive of apposition).

Keep faith with God. Believe in the power of Christ. Believe in the reality of your salvation. Trust him. Turn to him. Look to him, again and again and again.

Believe that God wants what's best for you.

Believe that God has placed you into permanent union with Christ, so that his blessings are your blessings. Believe that all things are possible in Christ.

Because the devil is fighting tooth and nail to make you turn anywhere but Christ. He wants you to lose faith. He wants you to forget faith. He wants you to despise faith and to say it doesn't work, or it's too hard for you to hold onto faith.

Here's where I want to blow your mind a little, and where I want to get off the same old track of how most people interpret the shield of faith.

So let's look at this familiar Scripture. I'm going to add my comments and reframe this thing as we go:

"Therefore we also, since we are surrounded by so great a cloud of witnesses [messed up people who kept faith anyway, listed in the previous chapter], let us lay aside every weight [needless additions to faith], and the sin [hostilities from Satan's Pain Machine] which so easily ensnares us, and let us run with endurance [ongoing faith] the race [*agōn*, struggle or gauntlet] that is set before us [by Satan], looking unto Jesus, the author and finisher of our faith, who for the joy that was set before Him [by God] endured the cross, despising the shame, and has sat down at the right hand of the throne of God." (Hebrews 12:1-2)

Here is where I made my own breakthrough while I've been studying for this book. I have always thought that the shield of faith meant a certain kind of faith: you have to have faith that God will handle your problems, regardless of the outcomes.

In other words, when you're talking about the shield of faith, most of us think about faith in God's ability to handle the problem that's facing us, faith in God's presence to deal with the situation, faith in God's providence to bring good out of evil and all that. In other words, when the fiery darts are flying thick and fast, the *object* of faith in that moment is God's ability to handle those specific fiery darts.

But if you're sick, do you have to believe that God will make you well? What if you simply don't believe?

Or if you're out of work, do you have to lift up the specific faith that God will pay your bills? What if you don't have that faith?

Or if you suffer depression, or if you feel deep anxiety, or if you struggle with sexual addiction or any addiction—does this mean that now you have to have faith that God will fix it, reverse it, deliver you, and all that?

Is that what the Shield of Faith is?

No. Because the precise object of faith is *not* that God's going to fix the problem that Satan's fiery darts shoot your way. Rather, the precise object of faith is over and over and over again the exact same thing.

What is the precise object of faith when hostilities come? When fiery darts are thick all around and fiery serpents have slithered into your tent?

The precise object of faith in any and every trial remains forever Jesus Christ, crucified and risen again! *Keep going back to Jesus and his Cross to remember again the love of God and the enormous cost of the grace that saved you! This is the faith of the Shield of Faith.*

Go back to the Cross. Go back to Calvary's Love. Go back to "Jesus loves me this I know, for the Bible tells me so." Go back to the day your faith began, and remember Him.

Go back to the forgiveness of sins through the sacrificial death of Christ.

Go back to the assurance that every blessing is yours and yours in abundance, for you're a joint heir with him.

Go back to that day when the Holy Spirit flooded in and sealed you in union with Christ forever.

Go back to that promise that sin shall not have dominion over you for you are not under law but under grace.

Go back to the promise that nothing in all creation can separate you from the love of God.

Go back to that victory when God in Christ more-than-conquered Satan and sin and death and depression and despair and every dark cloud hiding the radiance of his smiling face.

Look unto Jesus. Look unto the Savior.

Look and live.

Look and live again and again.

Look to him, and simply say,

> *Thank you Lord, for saving my soul.*
> *Thank you Lord, for making me whole.*
> *Thank you Lord, for giving to me,*
> *Thy great salvation, so rich and free.*

When your heart is so heavy you can't stand it, and when you're so anxious, and frustrated, and afraid, let faith grow by simply remembering the face of Jesus, and his shed blood, and his Cross, and a love that will not let you go, and a glory-land coming with no more sorrows and no more tears.

That is the shield of faith that all the hosts of hell combined can never get through. This is the faith that quenches the fiery darts, because this is the faith that lands you right back where you belong, in the *victory already won* for you by Jesus.

REFLECTION AND DISCUSSION

1. Rephrase in your own words the subject/object structure of faith. What do you think about this teaching?
2. Why is it important to say that faith is non-meritorious?
3. Saving faith is exclusive. Agree or disagree. Why? Support your position with Scripture.
4. When your faith is weak that God will solve a specific problem, you can still look to Jesus Christ. What might be some consequences when you do this?
5. According to Romans 3:26, who or what is the object of faith? What is the result of this faith in this object?

CHAPTER 11
THE FORMULA OF FAITH

The Christian is a born conqueror, the gates of hell shall not prevail against him. ~William Gurnall

FORGETTING THE OBVIOUS

"And when they had come to the multitude, a man came to Him, kneeling down to Him and saying, 'Lord, have mercy on my son, for he has seizures and suffers severely; for he often falls into the fire and often into the water. So I brought him to Your disciples, but they could not cure him.'" (Matthew 17:14-16)

Sometimes the devil scores points because we forget to do the obvious. Matthew shares an account of a man whose precious son is tormented by a demon. He brings the boy to the disciples of Jesus.

Sadly for the man and his son, in this section of Matthew, the disciples prove themselves to be clueless again and again. Essentially, they keep misunderstanding Jesus. They won't bring themselves to believe in a *crucified* Savior. Instead, they want a *victorious* Savior riding down from heaven to deliver Israel, knock Satan out, and make life great.

The disciples' confusion gets so bad that, just a chapter before this, Peter says something so stupid it's almost unbelievable. Peter actually rebukes Jesus for saying he will die on the Cross. Peter declares that Jesus will never suffer and die like that.

What a self-righteous parade of ignorance! Peter is literally attempting to cancel the one work by which Jesus will unleash God's grace and crush the devil. The disciples are hopelessly mired in their Cross-denying, Jesus-redefining, grace-crushing, self-righteous ways. What Peter said was so stupid, Jesus literally turns on him and basically says, "Shut up, Satan" TO PETER!

So, these are the malfunctioning disciples that this heartbroken father brings his demon-afflicted son to see. He says, "I brought him to your disciples but they could not cure him."

I'm sure the disciples imagine themselves to be something like King Arthur's Court. The Knights of the Round Table get to work on this poor boy. They command, but the demon does not obey. They bully the demon, but he laughs at them. They cry louder, but the demon just keeps humming a tune while torturing the boy. So they give up. They hand the boy back to his dad and turn to the next in line.

Epic fail.

The desperate father brings his suffering son to Jesus.

"Then Jesus answered and said, 'O faithless and twisted generation, how long shall I be with you? How long shall I bear with you? Bring him here to Me.' And Jesus rebuked the demon, and it came out of him; and the child was cured from that very hour." (Matthew 17:17-18)

Jesus is mad. I want you to understand something about the heart of Jesus, the heart of the Father, and the heart of the Spirit.

Jesus gets mad at the things that break your heart. He is upset at human suffering. And he's mad when his ministers fail to bring the healing powers of grace to a desperately hurting world.

In one simple rebuke, out comes the demon, and the little boy's demonic abuser is evicted. No more being thrown about like a rag doll by a demon. No more falling into fire and falling into water. Jesus does what the disciples could not, and he is exasperated that this kid had to suffer even one minute longer because of their failure.

> "Then the disciples came to Jesus privately and said, 'Why could we not cast it out?' So Jesus said to them, 'Because of your unbelief…'" (Matthew 17:19,20a)

The normal Greek word for faith is *pistis*. When you put an "a" in front of that word, it negates it: *apistis*. No faith. Lack of faith. Unbelief.

Why did the devil gain the upper hand? No faith. Not little faith, no faith.

I find this confusing. Is Jesus saying that of all the ways they used to try to expel the demon, they tried everything but faith?

Yes. That's exactly what he's saying. They forgot to do the obvious.

You can't outsmart the demons. You can't lawyer away the demons. You can't ritualize away the demons. No human power, no magic words, no incantation, no Gandalf's staff, and no human strength will ever make demons go away. If you come riding in like a Shining Knight on a steed and put any trust in yourself whatsoever, the devil's going to laugh in your face.

When those disciples went after that demon in their attempt to deliver that boy, they went right back into the same Cross-denying, Jesus-redefining, grace-crushing, self-righteous ways Jesus has been trying to get rid of their whole time with him.

Notice what they say: Why could *we* not cast it out? We? Us? I, me, my? Jesus would say, *Because you're not me. I do that, through my blood. And you don't get it yet.*

There's something incredibly powerful and beautiful hiding in plain sight in this story. I wonder if you saw it. I'm going to save that for chapter 15. You'll see.

But for now, let's just point out that Jesus assess the disciples as having "no faith." How can they miss something so obvious? Let's dig in.

1. Faith in yourself is no faith at all.

You might think they had faith, but it just wasn't enough faith. It wasn't big faith or strong faith. No, because look at what Jesus says next: "For assuredly, I say to you, if you have faith as a mustard seed, you will say to this mountain, 'Move from here to there,' and it will move; and nothing will be impossible for you'" (Matthew 17:20).

These mustard seeds are powdery little seeds. They're nothings. Jesus described them as the smallest of seeds (Mark 4:31). When Jesus compares faith to a mustard seed, he's saying it's not the size of faith that matters, it's the size of *who the faith is in*—the object of faith—that makes the difference.

It's not the size of the one who believes.

It's not the power of the one who believes.

It's not the virtue of the one who believes.

It's the size and power and virtue of the one who is *believed-in* that makes faith real.

When you put your faith in Jesus, that's the faith that moves mountains—meaning faith in Jesus Christ can move every obstacle the world, the flesh, and the devil raises up to block you from your abundant life of abundant grace.

Jesus has dedicated his school of discipleship to correcting his disciples' misplaced faith. The object of their faith was wrong. They trusted themselves. They trusted their status as FOJ (Friends of

Jesus). They even trusted Jesus, but only in his miracle-powers, and not in his real power, which is in his death and resurrection.

In return, the demons laughed at them.

So again and again Jesus urgently points their faith to the one and only object that makes faith real, which is Jesus-Christ-the-Savior-nailed-to-a-cross-and-risen-again.

And because they didn't get it, Jesus actually told them to stop talking about him. He wanted them to wait till they understood; to wait till he was risen again (Matthew 17:9)!

2. You can't have faith in Jesus the Conqueror without first having faith in Jesus the Crucified Savior.

The disciples' faith wasn't there yet. It makes no difference how big and blustery your faith might be, because want counts in faith is *always* the object.

When the object of your faith is the Lord Jesus Christ in the fulness of his person and work, then even one powdery speck of mustard seed faith will make the devil flee from you.

If we're going to have a shield constructed of molecules of faith, we have to get faith right.

THE FORMULA OF FAITH

Faith has a formula. Here it is. It is based on human nature. A human soul has three parts: mind, will, and emotions. Faith happens when all three parts respond to the Grace of Christ in the Gospel.

1. Emotions: your conscience convicts you that you are a sinner and you need a Savior.

Your conscience wakes you up to God. You don't need to be a theologian to know you fall short of God's moral standards. One look at the starry sky tells you there is a Creator who is bigger than you can imagine, better than you can please, and higher than you can reach by human power alone.

Your inner sense of God's moral laws combines with your inner awareness of your own imperfections to produce guilt and shame. In turn, guilt and shame produce a sense of need. You have a sin problem, and you need a Savior from your sins.

So, your emotions have become the first factor in the formula of faith. That's when the second factor kicks in.

2. Mind: your mind hears and understands that Jesus is that Savior, the only Savior, and the real crucified/risen again Savior.

You hear about Jesus. You hear that he died on the cross. You hear he died for a reason—Christ died for your sins.

Somebody explains that. Somebody explains the gospel to you. Somebody shows you it's not *your* works, it's *his* sacrifice. It's not your performance, it's his unmerited favor. It's not your religion and morality. It's his grace and love. It's not your human righteousness, for those are filthy rags. It's his perfect righteousness, given as a gift. It's not your self-sacrifice, it's his sacrifice on Calvary's Cross.

The truths of grace somehow get into your mind. The Holy Spirit helps you understand. The gospel becomes clear. As Moses lifted up the serpent in the wilderness, and as Jesus was lifted up on the Cross, you realize that the sin problem that is plaguing your conscience can only be solved by him. Those facts, those truths, those transcendent eternal realities, come into your mind, and the Spirit turns the lights on.

You realize it's true. You realize He's true. He's the One.

- You need a Savior, and it's Jesus.
- You need salvation, and he brings it.
- You need forgiveness, and he procured it on the Cross.

- You need heaven, and he opens it.
- You need a cleft in the rock to shield you from his holiness.
- You need a mighty object for your powerless faith and it is this bleeding dying Savior.

It's Jesus. It's Jesus plus nothing. Yes, you get it... you understand it. You believe it. So now your mind becomes the second factor in the formula of faith. Here comes the third factor.

3. Will: here you choose Jesus as your Personal Savior.

Will you say yes to Jesus? When Moses lifted up the serpent in the wilderness, the people were dying of snake bites. He put that bronze serpent on the pole, and sent out the word... Look and Live!

Their conscience told them, *Yes, I need this.*

Their mind told them, *Yes, this is true.*

So now their will has a choice to make. Will I go and look or not? That's the choice. That's the will, the volition, free will.

What if they *believed that* looking would save them, but they never went and looked? They would perish in their sins because they didn't *believe in* the divine solution.

It's not enough to believe the facts in your mind. A theologian would say that "mental assent" is not enough. You don't have the whole formula. Even the demons believe *that* Jesus is the Savior. They have mental assent (James 2:19).

But they have dug in their heels. They don't have the will to cast their hopes on him. (Not that demons could ever be saved, they're sealed in their doom, unlike you).

Saving faith is all three... mind plus will plus emotions* (*only enough to see your need of a Savior).

Saving faith is claiming him by personal faith, and relying exclusively upon Jesus, Crucified and Risen again, as your only hope for salvation.

So let's put the formula all together in an easily remembered way:

1. *Admit* — I am a sinner and I need a Savior. (Conscience/Emotions)
2. *Believe* — I believe that Jesus, by his shed blood on the Cross, is that Savior and the only Savior. (Mind)
3. *Choose* — I choose to trust Jesus as my only hope. (Will)

Faith is what happens when your whole soul responds to the amazing grace of God that comes to us from the Cross.

WHERE DOES FAITH COME FROM?

"So then faith comes by hearing, and hearing by the word of [Christ]." (Romans 10:17)

I put Christ in brackets, because that's what the Greek text actually says, and that's how all the modern translations translate it. The King James said "the word of God." But all the better Greek manuscripts say the Word of Christ.

What's the difference between the Word of God and the Word of Christ?

Nothing but emphasis.

- The Word of Christ is the Word of God as it emphasizes Christ.
- The Word of Christ is the message of grace.
- The Word of Christ is the new covenant teachings.
- The Word of Christ is the end of the Law as a way to God.
- The Word of Christ is Jesus smiling out from every page of Scripture.

- The Word of Christ is the Good News in Scripture as it has a basis in the finished Work of Christ.

Faith doesn't come when the preacher beats you up with the Bible. Faith doesn't come when the message crushes you with guilt and shame. Preaching the laws of God won't give you faith. Preaching that you need to stop this and start that won't give you faith. A lot of preachers preach the Word of God all around in circles and never preach the Word of Christ which is the Doctrine of Grace.

Paul asks, "This only I want to learn from you: Did you receive the Spirit by the works of the law, or by the hearing of faith?—" (Galatians 3:2). Notice the necessity of hearing.

Paul emphasizes hearing again in Romans: "…How shall they believe in Him of whom they have not *heard*? And how shall they *hear* without a preacher?" (Romans 10:14).

So here am I to write to you about the good news. Here am I to declare to you the good news of Christ. This is what God wants you to hear because this is what births faith your heart.

He wants you to hear again and again of the love of Christ which passes knowledge, so that God can't love you any more than he loves you right now. (Ephesians 3:19)

He wants you to hear that even on your very worst days, and even when you hate yourself and everybody else does too, the love of your Father in heaven doesn't even flicker.

He wants you to hear that "There is therefore now no condemnation for those who are in Christ Jesus" (Romans 8:1). No guilt or shame, no punishment or hell, not even a disapproving frown darkens the face of your Father in heaven, for your payment is complete in the finished work of Christ.

He wants you to hear that "God made him who knew no sin [Jesus] to be made sin for us [on the Cross] that we might be made the righteousness of God in him" (2 Corinthians 5:21). You are, therefore, perfect in his sight. Perfect on good days. Perfect on bad days. Perfect on holy days. Perfect on unholy days—when you're using again, nasty again, dirty again, or anything again, because he always sees you robed in the shimmering robes of the perfect righteousness of Christ.

Faith comes by hearing, and hearing by the Word of Christ. This good news is the Word of Christ.

He wants you to hear that God causes all things to work together for good to those who love him (Romans 8:28).

He wants you to hear that if God is for us, who can be against us (Romans 8:31).

He wants you to hear that "My God will supply all your need according to his riches in glory in Christ Jesus" (Philippians 4:19), and that Jesus has come that you might have life and that you might have it "more abundantly" (John 10:10).

He wants you to hear that once you're saved you're always saved, "For, what shall separate us from the love of God? Shall famine, or nakedness, or peril, or sword, or any other created thing? No, no, no. For nothing can separate us from the love of God which is in Christ Jesus our Lord" (paraphrased from Romans 8:28-39).

Where will you find your faith? Where does your faith come from? Where do Christians turn to load up material for the shield of faith?

Get yourself to the place again and again where you hear again and again the preaching and the teaching of the Word of Christ.

Hear the declaration of the Lamb of God who takes away the sin of the world... Who invites you to come boldly to the throne of grace to find mercy for every need... Because as far as the east is from the west, so far has he removed our transgression from us... So that once you're saved you're always saved, because no one will be able to pluck you out of your Father's hand... So that he now invites you, Come to me all who are weary and heavy laden, and I will give you rest... Which was purchased by the finished work of Jesus Christ, on Calvary's cross, once for all... So he will never leave you or forsake you… So you can shout to the heavens: We are more than conquerors through him who loved us… And… I can do all things through Christ who gives me strength.

And when the fiery darts are thick around us, we can hear God say, "Fear not, for I am with you; Be not dismayed, for I am your God. I will strengthen you, Yes, I will help you, I will uphold you with My righteous right hand" (Isaiah 41:10).

Let us be found looking unto Jesus… the author of our faith, the Rock of ages, cleft for me.

REFLECTION AND DISCUSSION

1. How do you think Peter felt when Jesus called him Satan? Was that harsh? Why or why not?
2. Can you think of some times when you forgot to do the obvious—pray, turn to God, turn to Scriptures, ask for prayer from your friends—in a tough situation? Why do you think this might happen?
3. "You can't have faith in Jesus the Conqueror without first having faith in Jesus the Crucified Savior." What are your thoughts about this?
4. The Formula of Faith says Mind plus Will plus Emotions equals Faith. What are your thoughts about this? What does this mean for people who believe in their minds but never choose Jesus in their wills (free will, personal choice)?
5. In 1 Peter 5:8,9 what are Peter's instructions on how to resist the devil?

CHAPTER 12
THE HELMET OF SALVATION

One affirmative from God's mouth for thy pardoned state carries more weight than a thousand negatives from Satan's.
~William Gurnall

SPIRITUAL PROBLEMS REQUIRE SPIRITUAL SOLUTIONS

"And take the helmet of salvation…" (Ephesians 6:17)

We live in an age of anxiety. We live in an age of high stress. Counselors and therapists report rising levels of depression, discouragement, and despair. Mental illness and emotional brokenness are on the rise. Addictions. Dysfunctions. Substance abuse. Anxiety disorders. Struggling marriages. Loneliness.

Studies say that the rates of depression skyrocketed by 25% in the first year of the pandemic. Enforced isolation comes with a higher price tag than those who required it ever contemplated. I have talked to teachers who say they feel all they're doing right now is cleaning up a mess.

I have to imagine the devil, sitting in his hellish chambers, surrounded by his mightiest principalities, pouring diabolical champagne, laughing, and raising a toast to the astounding success of their despicable campaign of human destruction and despair in our society, in our day.

Don't think for a minute, that the hopelessness we see is simply of human, or even biological, origin. No, no, no! Those things play a part, but it's deeper than that. That despicable fallen angel—that dark lord, Satan—His Infernal Majesty, is working his plan of hatred against the human race. He's striking back against God.

Never forget where the sadness comes from.

Because if these problems were *simply* of human origin, we could look for human solutions. But this sadness, this despair is the devil's acid spit raining down on us. We wrestle—we engage in close quarters, hand-to-hand, close-enough-to-smell-his-nasty-breath combat—against spiritual hosts of wickedness in the heavenly places.

Problems in the Spirit realm require solutions in the Spirit realm.

When our emotional struggles are rooted in spiritual warfare, it's time to make sure we have on the Helmet of Salvation.

THE HELMET OF SALVATION

First let's talk about about the *helmet* and then about *salvation*.

Roman soldiers wore helmets. These were made either of metal or of hardened leather. The purpose was obvious: to protect the head. The enemy armies would shoot their arrows, hurl their rocks, and throw their spears but the head would be protected. Even the blow of a sword, landing on the helmet, would be deflected, giving the soldier time to attack his enemy and save his life.

The head is the seat of thought and emotions, and this is the devil's primary attack.

The devil is attacking your mind. He assaults your mental health every way he can. The stuff you are dealing with that brings you down is not just situational. It's not just relational. It's not just random. It's not just biological. It's not just the consequences of your own dumb choices.

We wrestle not against flesh and blood.

Demons work through philosophies. They work through deceptions. They work through worldviews. They work through temptations. They work through stuff that looks enticing, but has a very sharp hook in it.

Demons create strongholds of false belief. They don't just target your morality, where they're trying to get you to sin. They do that but they do more than that. They target every aspect of your mind. What you think, what you believe, how you feel. Do you have any clue how much the Bible talks about mental health?

Everything the Bible says about love, joy, and peace. Everything the Bible says about hope. About marriage and dating and relationships. About sexuality. About parenting. Even about finances and physical healing. All of the invitations to pray. All of the beautiful teachings about the love of the Father in heaven. All of these things, and so much more are for your mental and emotional and spiritual health.

In other words, your helmet.

To put one word on all of it… the helmet of… what?

All of this is wrapped up in the ultimate gift and the unparalleled blessing called *salvation*.

Salvation is your helmet. So, using Paul's analogy, salvation is what protects your head, and that means mental health.

Mark's gospel offers a powerful, and extreme, illustration of the demonic attack on mental health.

> "And when He had come out of the boat, immediately there met Him out of the tombs a man with an unclean spirit, who had his

dwelling among the tombs; and no one could bind him, not even with chains, because he had often been bound with shackles and chains. And the chains had been pulled apart by him, and the shackles broken in pieces; neither could anyone tame him. And always, night and day, he was in the mountains and in the tombs, crying out and cutting himself with stones." (Mark 5:2-5)

Here is this poor man, matted in his own filth, utterly broken, and completely out of his mind. This was caused by the devil!

At the end of his story you will see what salvation through Jesus Christ can do for a person's mental health. Let's break it down.

SIX WAYS SALVATION SAFEGUARDS YOUR MENTAL HEALTH

1. Salvation delivers you from guilt and shame.

No functioning human soul can escape its own conscience. This is part of us having been created in the image of God. There's a little machine inside of you that knows right from wrong. That little machine also tells you that somewhere somehow the scales of justice must be balanced.

The Bible calls God, "The Judge of all" (Hebrews 12:23). The human heart instinctively knows this.

Guilt is that nagging sense that you've done something wrong in the sight of the Judge of All. Of all of the teachings in the Bible, the one that is most obviously true and beyond all argument is this: "For all have sinned and come short of the glory of God" (Romans 3:23).

Guilt and shame make a lot of things go haywire inside your soul. They make you avoid closeness. They make you hide. They make you wear masks, so that other people can never see—and potentially reject—the real you.

Guilt and shame break down relationships. They damage your

sex life. They make people act out in ways that are contrary to their own nature. They make you do stuff you don't want to do but can't stop doing, like the man among the tombs.

Here is this poor man dwelling among the tombs. Crying out. Isolated. Who will deliver him from the demonic strongholds of guilt and shame? Who will look into the darkness and filth of his damaged heart and wash his sins as white as snow?

Answer: only Jesus!

The beautiful thing about salvation is it brings total forgiveness for all your sins, past, present, and future.

If you have salvation, do you realize that there is not even one speck of the tiniest sin on your record? Do you realize that everything bad has been wiped from your record? Do you realize that every evil thought, word, and deed has been lifted out of you and transferred to Jesus Christ hanging on the cross? "Behold! The Lamb of God who takes away the sin of the world!" (John 1:29).

> **In theology this is called *Atonement*.**
> **It means that God took away your sins when Jesus died on the cross.**

No amount of secular therapy can erase your sins. There is no medication, and no spiritual practice, that can wash your sins away. Only Jesus, and only the salvation he brings, can end the tyranny of guilt in your life.

Put on the Helmet of Salvation, and believe that guilt and shame have no power over you.

2. Salvation removes the internal drive toward punishment and self-punishment.

The man among the tombs is so broken emotionally that the Bible says he spent his days crying out and cutting himself with stones.

For some people, this is just so on the nose—please let God's Spirit show you yourself here. You may not be cutting, but what other forms of self-sabotage might you have? What other forms of self punishment might you be engaging in?

Is it relational? Is it financial? Is it in your own health? A string of regrettable choices? Are you punishing others as surrogates for your own guilt?

The same conscience that convicts you of your sin also convinces you that sin must be punished. Thank God for Jesus!

> THE SAME CONSCIENCE THAT CONVICTS YOU OF YOUR SIN ALSO CONVINCES YOU THAT SIN MUST BE PUNISHED. THANK GOD FOR JESUS!

The only thing that secular counselors can do is to try to define sin as not sin. They alleviate guilt by basically saying, "Don't feel guilty." The only way this makes sense and even pretends to work, is if you harden your heart to your conscience. The devil is all for this strategy.

Even if you define your most heinous sin as not a sin—even if you justify it, even if you rationalize it, even if you actually redefine it as something good—you can't lie to your own soul. And you certainly can't lie to God.

Evil must be punished or the cosmos is out of balance in the end. Sin must be paid for or the universe is, at its core, unrighteous.

From the very first sacrifice in the Garden of Eden, when God made coats of skin for Adam and Eve, right on down through today the truth will never go away that, "Without the shedding of blood there is no remission" of sins (Hebrews 9:22).

Your soul knows this. But without Jesus, who are you going to punish?

The devil loves it when you punish yourself. He loves self-atonement. The demons will point you to anyone and anything but Jesus Christ crucified for you as the punishment for sin.

So, here this poor man was shedding his own blood. There are tribes and religions all around the world that call for the shedding of blood. Even if they don't shed blood, they still call for some form of self-sacrifice, self-payment, or self-punishment.

This happens not only religiously, but psychologically too. So many people actually hurt themselves again and again, and they don't know why. What's happening is they are acting out the inescapable truth that sin must be punished, and they're turning that drive inward on themselves.

Others turn that drive outward. They lash out at others. They act out in violence, whether that's physical, verbal, or emotional. They make other people pay the price in a broken attempt to atone for sins.

Who can deliver us from this drive toward punishment? Who can make us mentally whole?

Only Jesus and the salvation he brings. Soon, our man among the tombs will encounter the Savior. And what an utter transformation we will see!

Jesus was punished for our iniquities. He was punished for our sins. All the penalty fell on him. Your forgiveness is not a fiction, it is an absolute reality founded upon the bedrock of the sacrifice and the finished work of Jesus Christ on Calvary's cross.

Do you want punishment? Look to Christ on the Cross.

Do you want a penalty to be paid? Look to the cross.

Do you want the scales of justice balanced on your behalf? Look to the Lamb of God who takes away the sin of the world.

Do you want freedom from the inner drive to hurt yourself, sacrifice yourself, or punish yourself and others?

Then look long and hard at your bloodied Savior nailed to that cross and listen to him say IT IS FINISHED!

> **In theology this is called *Expiation*.**
> **It means that God punished Christ for your sins instead of punishing you.**

The devil hates Expiation. He attacks this doctrine all the time. If he can confuse you on Christ's payment for your sin, he can catch you without your helmet and bash you in the head.

We are talking about the helmet of salvation, meaning God's foundation for mental wholeness and health. I am saying that the deeper you embrace the salvation you already possess as a child of God, the more your soul will be healed of the scars and dysfunctions of the devil's fallen world.

3. Salvation ends the need to prove your worth.

On the day that you were saved, assuming you are saved—and you might not be, in which case you can get saved today—something happens so remarkable that the angels are still amazed and the demons just don't know what to do.

On the day that you were saved not only did God take away your sins through atonement, and not only did he punish all your sins through expiation, he also did something else.

God lavished upon you the most remarkable treasure in all the cosmos. God actually gave you the pure and perfect righteousness of Christ.

Righteousness means goodness. Specifically righteousness means goodness that is good enough for God.

But there is another factor of righteousness that you really need to understand. *Righteousness is the landing pad for the blessing of God.*

God doesn't bless unrighteousness. He can't, or he would contradict his own character. Even if you're another Mother Theresa on steroids, you can never meet the righteous standards of God.

- Paul says there is none righteous no not one (Romans 3:10).
- He also says there is no one who does good no not one (Romans 3:12)
- King Solomon declares there is not a just person upon the earth who does good and sins not (Ecclesiastes 7:20).

In comes the great gift of divine righteousness from God to you. This happens when you are saved. In that split second, God adds his own righteousness to you. He robes you in the shimmering robes of the righteousness of Christ. "[That I may] be found in Him, not having my own righteousness, which is from the law, but that which is through faith in Christ, the righteousness which is from God by faith" (Philippians 3:9).

As soon as God gives his righteousness to you, he convenes the Supreme Court of heaven. The Judge of the universe looks upon you and sees nothing but divine righteousness. God in heaven, therefore, declares that you are righteous, and he tells the angels, the demons, the devil, and the world that you are officially good enough for God for all the ages of eternity!

So much sadness is caused by broken self-esteem.

So much discouragement comes from feeling that you have no worth.

So much depression comes from trying to answer the criticisms of your past, even from people who are long dead, who said that you would never amount to anything.

Yet here is God to say that you are righteous. To say that you are good enough for him. To say that you are perfect in his sight, and are beautiful, and that you are the righteousness of God in Christ.

If God is for you, who can be against you?

In theology, this is called *Justification*.
It means that God declares you perfectly, eternally *righteous* when you believe in Jesus.

Satan hates justification. He has launched all out war on this doctrine. It's one of the key teachings in all of Scripture. Sadly, the devil's attack is frequently successful.

In the early centuries of Christianity, the doctrine of justification by faith was largely forgotten by the main bulk of church leadership. Here and there, there were always pockets that taught it, but this gracious doctrine got buried under an avalanche of meaningless ritual and performance-based legalism.

In the 16th century, a young Catholic monk got tired of this ritual and legalism. He had spent a lifetime, sweating and straining to establish his own righteousness by his own good works. But he knew it was a losing battle. One day, the Word of God jumped out at him. He finally realized that his righteousness could only come from God. "The just [righteous] will live by faith," he realized (Habakkuk 2:4, quoted in Romans 1:17 and Galatians 3:11). Not works. Not ritual. Not sacraments. Faith.

When this monk, named Martin Luther, unburied justification by faith from Satan's avalanche of lies, he launched a Reformation in the Church. Luther also experienced nothing but spiritual warfare. When you take your stand here, on the imputed righteousness of Christ, the devil will fight you too.

But if you keep on believing, he will flee from you. And, as a bonus, you can live the rest of your days with nothing left to prove. And if that doesn't give you psychological wholeness, nothing will.

So, say it out loud: "I am the righteousness of God." Say it often, especially when the devil whispers it isn't true.

4. Salvation bestows God's love and grace.

Why did that demon possessed man live among the tombstones? Why was he there, all alone, matted in his own filth? When people came to help, tend, and feed him, he lashed out at them. He attacked those who would love him. He had to be restrained, for his own benefit. But the demonic power in him broke those shackles over and over again.

I looked at a research study about men in prison. The researchers wanted to know why these men did what they did. Why they did these crimes. What drove them and what motivated them.

When they dug deep enough they came to an answer that probably doesn't surprise you. Love.

The ultimate dysfunction is feeling unloved.

The ultimate salvation is the love of God poured out in your heart. God declares, "Yes, I have loved you with an everlasting love; Therefore with lovingkindness [grace] I have drawn you" (Jeremiah 31:3).

If you're a Christian, God loves you to the maximum right now. He's not waiting for you to be a better Christian. He's not waiting for you to be a better human. He's not waiting for you to pay a price, prove yourself, or anything else.

God can't love you anymore than he loves you right now. His love is infinite. His love is perfect. His love is permanent. His love is tender and compassionate. When you die and go to heaven, and stand before him face-to-face, even then his love will be no more than it already is today.

In theology, this is called *Propitiation*.
It means that God's justice is so satisfied with you that God's love must be lavished on you.

John tells us, "In this is love, not that we loved God, but that He loved us and sent His Son to be the propitiation for our sins" (1 John 4:10). No one else might be satisfied with you. You might not be satisfied with yourself. But God is. Having put your faith in Jesus, you are saved, and in that salvation, God loves you with a perfect love.

Nothing can separate you from his love. Nothing can diminish his love. Not even your worst sin on your worst day.

- Jesus loved him among the tombs.
- Jesus loved him with his smell.
- Jesus loved him with his violence.
- Jesus loved him with his demons.
- Jesus loved him with his cursings.
- Jesus loved him in his isolation.
- Jesus loved him in his madness.
- Jesus loves him in his self-loathing.
- Jesus loved him when he was cutting himself.
- Jesus loved him when he was in shackles.
- Jesus loved him when he was in bondage to the darkest forces imaginable.

Why? Because all those things, Jesus paid for. Jesus absorbed. Jesus took the hit for them.

All so that he could make it possible for a holy God to love an ungodly sinner like this poor man, who is just an unpolished version of us today. "In all their affliction He was afflicted, And the Angel of His Presence saved them; In His love and in His pity He redeemed them; And He bore them and carried them All the days of old" (Isaiah 63:9).

Salvation is the boundless streams of the love of God flowing into the heart and mind of anyone who simply believes. Salvation is abundance, healing, wholeness, and every good gift that a loving father could ever conceive of giving to a beloved daughter or son.

No one can put a price on it other than the finished work of Christ.

Once you are under its healing streams, your blessing is assured.

Jesus seeing this afflicted man—and knowing that soon, on an old rugged Cross, he would bear in his own body that man's demonic addictions and mental afflictions—braved a storm at sea to come and love this man that nobody could love.

He set him free. "Then they came to Jesus, and saw the one who had been demon-possessed and had the legion [of demons], sitting and clothed and in his right mind…" (Mark 5:15).

He had been running and hiding day and night in the mountains and in the tombs, but now he was sitting.

He had been naked and filthy, but now he was clothed.

He had been out of his mind, but now he was in his right mind, healthy, whole, and sane.

This is the Helmet of Salvation. This is mental health leading to spiritual, physical, relational, and every other kind of wholeness and blessing.

This is the salvation you already have, Christian, ever since you first believed.

5. Salvation reanimates your dead spiritual core, reconnecting you to God and his blessings.

Sin broke you. Salvation fixed you.

The main break is something called *spiritual death.*

Every person is born into this world in a state of spiritual death. That means that our very being is damaged. We are less than we were made to be—body, soul, spirit, mind, will, and emotions.

Everything is twisted. Your body carries pain and will die. Your soul is messed up. Your mind is mostly shut down. Your will is weak where it should be strong and strong where it should be weak. Your emotions can turn dark and bitter. Your spirit is shriveled up and dead.

People say that spiritual death means separation from God. That is the most common definition, but it falls far short of what spiritual death really means.

> "And you He made alive, who were dead in trespasses and sins, in which you once walked according to the course of this world, according to the prince of the power of the air, the spirit who now works in the sons of disobedience, among whom also we all once conducted ourselves in the lusts of our flesh, fulfilling the desires of the flesh and of the mind, and were by nature children of wrath, just as the others." (Ephesians 2:1-3)

Spiritual death is a coin with two sides: a personal side and a judicial side.

The *personal* side is a dead and unresponsive spirit and the corruption of your very being.

The *legal* side is condemnation from the justice of God. It's not just that a person is separated from God, they're actually under the wrath of God!

This is spiritual death.

Under spiritual death, there is something so broken inside you that, before God Almighty, you are dead in trespasses and sins. You are under the influence of the demons and devil, you are entrapped again and again by the lusts of the flesh, you are guilty of running a godless agenda, and you are, *by nature*, a child of wrath.

Scripturally speaking, before Christ enters our lives, we're the Walking Dead. We're snack food for demons.

Spiritual death doesn't stop at wrecking our relationship with God; it damages *every* relationship. It is the malfunction squatting in the darkness behind every hatred, addiction, dysfunction, and cruelty. It is the fundamental breakdown of human nature. Spiritual death normalizes life among the tombstones.

In comes Jesus to resolve this situation. He knows all about this. He knows all about you. He loves you, so he says, "Do not marvel that I said to you, 'You must be born again'" (John 3:7).

Born once, die twice. Born twice, die once. Born once—physically but not spiritually—die twice—physical death plus eternal death forever.

Born twice—born physically and then born again spiritually, meaning you're saved—then you die once—you'll die physically, but that's just transportation to heaven.

When you were born again, God saved you.

In that moment, God swooped in by his Holy Spirit. He went down to your circuit breakers to turn back on every switch that had been turned off by the Fall.

He took that dead old spirit of yours and made it alive again. For the first time since the day you were born, you are now both physically alive *and* spiritually alive too.

In theology this is called *Regeneration*.
It means that God makes your spirit alive and reactivates all the God-given powers your soul was created with.

This is spiritual rebirth. This is what it means to be born again. "Not by works of righteousness which we have done, but according to His mercy He saved us, through the washing [cleansing power] of regeneration and renewing of the Holy Spirit" (Titus 3:5).

Regeneration is a radical change. There is an absolutely radical difference between saved and not saved. No one is "kind-of" born. You've either been born or not born. There are no shades of gray here. It's an on/off switch.

Regeneration is immediate. It is complete. It is perfect. It is supernatural.

You have a new nature. You are a new creation. Regeneration creates a brand new spiritual species. You are a different person on the day after you are saved than you were the day before.

In comes the devil to say, "You're all on your own." But since you're born again, you can say, "I have a Father who is with me, my God who is for me, and my help is only a prayer away."

The devil will say, "People don't change. Can a leopard change its spots?" But the born-again person can say, "You're wrong, devil, because you are looking at a New Creation, and I am being transformed day by day, just by learning more and more about Jesus."

The devil whispers, "It's not real, you know. It's only make-believe." But regeneration makes you say, "Oh, you poor devil, I have God's Word in my mind and God's witness in my heart that I am his child, and you'll never take that away."

The devil will shout, "Ha! Look at you! You sinned again!" And your heart will say, "I know. I shouldn't have. But I am still the righteousness of God in Christ, and it's totally different now. Because I'm beginning to love God more than my sins, because the one who has been forgiven much loves much."

And when the devil says, "You can't," the born-again person can shout, "I can do all things through Christ, who gives me strength!"

Are you saved?

Good. Then wear your helmet.

6. Salvation sets you free from spiritual bondage to every dark force and unleashes the truest self God created you to be.

God made you for dominion. God made you with authority and power. God made you to be free. There should be no one over you, mentally, emotionally, or spiritually, but the Lord Jesus Christ.

But sin wrecked all of that. Sin enslaved you. I'm not talking about this or that sin that you committed. I'm talking about sin in the world, sin in the Garden of Eden, resulting in sin invading the deepest guts of your soul, like a nasty parasite, sucking everything out of you all the time. In theology it is called Original Sin, and because of this:

- Sin is your master.
- Addiction is your master.
- Dysfunction is your master.
- Mental brokenness is your master.

- Satan is your master.
- Death is your master.
- Hell is your master.

When the Bible talks about slavery and about bondage, it's using something literal to talk about something spiritual. The equivalent today of slavery and bondage would be the words, addiction, and dysfunction.

- Jesus answered them, "Most assuredly, I say to you, whoever commits sin is a slave of sin." (John 8:34)
- That through death He might destroy him who had the power of death, that is, the devil, and release those who through fear of death were all their lifetime subject to bondage. (Hebrews 2:14-15)

Sins are not just random acts of badness. Sins are an existential crisis of being stuck in captivity to an evil master.

We need someone to set us free. Guess who that someone is!

The Bible gives us a powerful illustration of our deliverance.

HOSEA AND GOMER

"When the LORD began to speak by Hosea, the LORD said to Hosea: 'Go, take yourself a wife of harlotry And children of harlotry, For the land has committed great harlotry By departing from the LORD.' So he went and took Gomer the daughter of Diblaim, and she conceived and bore him a son." (Hosea 1:2-3)

This is weird. God has a prophet—a religious spokesperson. His name is Hosea. God actually tells him to marry a prostitute.

So Hosea marries Gomer, the prostitute. They have a son. Then they have a daughter. Then they have another son. God is using all of this to help Hosea teach the people about his grace, and about the high price of rejecting his grace. Happy couple. Grace personified. This lasted a couple of years.

But then, Gomer goes back to her old ways. She abandons Hosea and her kids. She actually gets back into the old business and spirals downward super fast. This is the high price of sin. This is the high price of misusing grace and redefining grace.

Gomer sinks so low, she descends into slavery. Soon, she finds herself in shackles, literally in the slave market with a "For Sale" sign around her neck.

The devil has her right where he wants her. Swamped by her own sin. Broken and ruined. Unloved, turned into an object, and being sold to the highest bidder.

She is an emblem of every person who isn't saved.

All she could do was to wait for the next master to buy her and use her. Surrounded by filth, the smell of death, the weeping of slaves, and the clanking of chains, all hope was gone.

But then she heard that last sound she could ever imagine.

She heard a familiar voice—a voice from her past. "Gomer," he said. There was a tenderness there she hadn't heard for years.

Gomer looked up, and saw. There, standing ankle deep in the filth of the slave market was the man who loved her without limits. The man she cheated on, and ran away from.

There stood her own husband, Hosea—the prophet, the man of God—at the slave's auction block.

Hosea looked at the handler. "Name your price," he said. Without flinching, Hosea paid that price in full. He bought his wife back to himself, at great cost.

This is what he wrote: "Then the LORD said to me, 'Go and get your wife again. Bring her back to you and love her, even though she loves adultery...' So I bought her back for fifteen pieces of silver and about five bushels of barley and a measure of wine" (Hosea 3:1, 2, NLT).

Here's the most amazing thing of that moment. He did not buy her as a slave. He did not buy her as a servant. He did not even buy her as a wife. He bought her as a person. He paid the price, not to own her, but to set her free.

In the Bible, this is called *Redemption*.
It means that Jesus paid the price to buy us and to set us free from every dark force that would dominate our lives, once for all.

I am talking about a Helmet of Salvation which is forged in the fires of redemption.

Redemption means to buy a slave and set them free. You were shackled in that slave market too. You were a slave to sin, a slave to death, a slave to Satan, and a slave to hell, and a slave to the flesh (your own fallen nature). But Jesus set you free from all of it.

The important thing to know is he didn't set you free by *power* only, but by *payment*. That is what redeem means. Redemption means to pay a price. It means to buy back. This wasn't an arm wrestling match, but a satisfaction of penalty and debt. This was the payment, the ransom, the total elimination of any debt to any dominating force.

Jesus didn't just pry the prison doors open; he paid the debt so fully that divine justice actually required the prisoner be set free. Your salvation wasn't a jailbreak; it was the payment of all that God's holiness demanded.

What was the payment price? The payment price was the shed blood of Jesus in his sacrificial death on the Cross, "knowing that you were not redeemed with corruptible things, like silver or gold... but with the precious blood of Christ, as of a lamb without blemish and without spot" (1 Peter 1:18-19).

Can you even begin to imagine that kind of love?

Jesus Christ did not buy you to boss you around: he bought you to set you free.

He bought you to restore your dominion and right to be a royal, happy, free, beloved, empowered, beautiful, accepted, radiant, blessed, provided for, secure, heir of God and joint heir with Jesus.

Sin is not the boss of you. Temptation is not the boss of you. Depression is not the boss of you. Your peers are not the boss of you. The things that make you ashamed are not the boss of you. Your failures are not the boss of you. Your disabilities are not the boss of you. Your anger is not the boss of you. Your enemies, your ex, your losses, your failures, your heartbreaks, your addictions, your dysfunctions, your illnesses, your mental illnesses, your debt, your fears, your weirdness, you're anything else you can think of, is not the boss of you.

Satan is not the boss of you.

Demons are not the boss of you.

Evil is not the boss of you.

Redemption means that *you* are the boss of you, under the mighty lordship of Jesus Christ

Has your marriage fallen into a trap? Jesus wants to redeem your marriage, and buy both you and your partner back to himself and each other.

Has your financial life collapsed far from God? The redeeming power of the blood of Christ can apply even there — and lift you out of whatever financial prison you have made for yourself.

Maybe you need sexual redemption—deliverance from the emotional prison of exploitation, or porn, or uncommitted sexual expression, or social contagion, or any twisted distortion of God's design for sex.

Maybe your heart is a tangled mess of addictions: drugs, alcohol, gambling, or the cruel master called narcissism.

Or maybe your job is a jungle, and you feel trapped by golden handcuffs in a den of vipers.

Whatever jail holds you, Jesus Christ has purchased you out of it. If nothing else, at least your heart, mind, and emotions are free to soar. Christian, say it: *I am redeemed!*

There is no price too high for him.

There is no prison too strong for him.

There is no hole too deep for him.

There is no demon too strong for him.

You are free.

You are not a *sinner*, you are a *saint* who struggles with sin.

You are not an *addict*, you are a *Christian* who struggles with addiction.

You are not a *victim*, you are *more than a conqueror* and, yes, you have your battles. But *redemption* is the deepest truth about you.

There's a difference between the thing you are and the things you struggle with.

The thing you are is *redeemed*, and the things you struggle with will fade away if you only do one thing

Always name your *identity* by your redemption, and label your *behaviors* by what you do.

Why? Why should you do that? Because the Bible tells you to wear the Helmet of Salvation to shield you from all the attacks of Satan.

MENTAL HEALTH IS YOUR BIRTHRIGHT

In all of the struggles and battles and warfare of life, having salvation is your biggest and strongest and most fundamental defense.

The devil wants you discouraged. The devil wants you frustrated. The devil wants you angry, addicted, depressed, and, if he can, suicidal.

The ultimate dysfunction is feeling unloved.

> THE ULTIMATE DYSFUNCTION IS FEELING UNLOVED.

The ultimate salvation is the love of God poured out in your heart, which fixes every other love.

This is exactly where the devil is fighting you.

So when St Paul here tells you wear your helmet, it is because the Helmet of Salvation is God's way of safeguarding your mental health.

Two things can be equally true.

One is that the teachings of Jesus are the most psychologically healthy truths ever given on planet earth. Whether you're looking for peace, for self-acceptance, for relationships, for forgiveness, power, purpose, success, sobriety, love, or any other aspect of mental health, there is nothing that even comes close to biblical Christianity.

The second is that the psychological brilliance of Jesus is superglued to the deep theology of Jesus and his Cross. You can't separate them. In fact, the deeper you go into the theology the stronger you will be in your psychology when the devil comes to hit you in the head.

To be clear, I'm not trying to psychologize our theology. I'm trying to theologize our psychology by setting it on the grace of Christ, through the Cross of Christ, in opposition to the demonic onslaught of the dark side.

HOW DO YOU WEAR YOUR HELMET?

You put on the helmet of salvation, like every other piece of armor, by declaring faith in Jesus and his finished work on the Cross, *in the very moment* of your struggle.

So the bottle tugs at you, or the porn tempts you, or the demons wave your addictions in front of your face. In that moment you declare, *I am redeemed by the blood of the Lamb and you have no power over me!* This is the faith it takes to walk (or run) away.

The weakness surfaces, and you feel inadequate. In that moment you declare, *I am born again, regenerated, and a new creation in Christ, so I can do all things through him who gives me strength.*

The voice in your head says, I'm a loser, and the bullies in your life say, you don't matter. In that moment, you declare, *Jesus is my propitiation! And if God is satisfied with me, I don't care what anyone else thinks.*

Inferiority rises up, and so workaholism and perfectionism rise up too. The drive to prove yourself, wears you out. The fear of failure runs your life. But in that moment you declare, *I am the righteousness of God, for I am justified once for all by Jesus. I can live with nothing left to prove.*

A depraved voice comes in to say you have to punish yourself, and you see patterns of self destruction, and self defeat emerging. That's when you can say, *All the punishment I'll ever deserve has already fallen on Christ. He is my expiation and that work is complete.* Wear your helmet by faith.

When the devil punches you with guilt and shame. Just point him to the Cross and declare, *Be silent Devil! I stand upon the atonement and the finished work of Christ.*

I pray your helmet shines bright and strong as you dig deeper into the wonders of your triumphant salvation in Jesus Christ.

REFLECTION AND DISCUSSION

1. Why is the Helmet of Salvation a perfect illustration of mental health?
2. Of the six ways that salvation safeguards your mental health, which one or two speak to your heart most deeply? Why?
3. "The ultimate dysfunction is feeling unloved." What are your thoughts and feelings about this statement?
4. How have you seen the devil attacking love in your life or in the lives of people you care about?

5. What does 1 Corinthians 6:11 say about what God has done for you now that you are saved? How does this affect your identity?

NOTE: If you desire to polish up your Helmet of Salvation by digging deeper into the wonderful salvation doctrines in this chapter, I have written a book about them. It is called *The Cross,* and you can find it on Amazon here: https://amzn.to/444U78D

CHAPTER 13
THE SWORD OF THE SPIRIT, PART 1

A pilot without his chart, a scholar without his book, and a soldier without his sword, are alike ridiculous. But, above all these, it is absurd for one to think of being a Christian, without knowledge of the Word of God and some skill to use this weapon.
~William Gurnall

A HUNDRED TALL MEN

THE YEAR IS 1861, and a fledgling America is plunging into the Civil War. At the same time, a world away, on islands remote even from New Zealand, two missionaries are awakened by a loud commotion. They hear men outside their primitive thatched hut. The men are chanting to their gods, calling for the death of the missionaries.

John Paton, and Mary Ann Robson Paton, husband and wife, peered through their small window. They saw that scores of hostile islanders have surrounded the station with torches. They intended to burn the place down and to kill the missionary couple. Worst of

THE CHRISTIAN IN COMPLETE ARMOR   175

all, this was a cannibalistic tribe. They had already feasted on the flesh of other missionaries before the Patons.

The Patons got down on their knees and prayed throughout the night, asking God to deliver them.

Their prayer focused on the words of Jesus in Matthew 28:20: "Behold, I am with you always, even to the end of the world."

Actually, they were at the end of the world. That promise that Christ would be with them even there, was John Paton's life-verse. He proclaimed it over and over gain throughout his harrowing adventures as a missionary.

To them, it was the Word of God.

To them, it was a word of God's presence and word of God's protection.

Now, their lives are on the edge. They will not survive the night.

The tense, dark hours passed, yet the islanders kept their distance. They were still chanting, but strangely growing quieter.

Finally, around daybreak, the Patons looked out the window again. They couldn't believe their eyes. The hostile tribesmen were gone. John Paton was baffled. There seemed to be nothing preventing the islanders from attacking, yet no attack came.

These men were cannibals who had already massacred other missionaries and eaten their flesh. Why were he and his wife spared?

Paton didn't find out why the islanders left so mysteriously until a year later. That's when the chief of the tribe became a Christian. Remembering that siege a year before, the missionaries asked the newly converted chief what happened. "Why did you leave before you burned our station to the ground? Why did you spare our lives?"

The chief replied, "We were afraid of the men who were with you."

"Men?" Paton said. "What men?"

The chief said, "There were a hundred tall men around your house that night. Their clothing shined with light, and they had swords in their hands. We knew that they would never let us harm you, so we went back to our village." [Source: Ray Stedman, *Spiritual Warfare,* raystedman.org]

"Behold, I am with you always, even to the end of the world" (Matthew 28:20). That was the Word of God to them.

THE SWORD OF THE SPIRIT

The Devil hates the Word of God. The Word of God is the devil's kryptonite.

1. BATTLEFIELD - the fiercest battlefield in the cosmic conflict is the terrain of the believer's heart and mind.

The mind is the battlefield. As we have seen, this is where the war is fought. It is the very real inner world of mind, heart, psychology, and soul.

So Satan works overtime to raise up strongholds across the battlefield of your mind.

- "This *wisdom* does not descend from above, but is earthly, sensual, demonic." (James 3:15)
- "Now the Spirit expressly says that in latter times some will depart from *the faith,* giving heed to deceiving spirits and *doctrines* of demons," (1 Timothy 4:1)
- "But I fear, lest somehow, as the serpent deceived Eve by his craftiness, so your *minds* may be corrupted from the simplicity that is in Christ." (2 Corinthians 11:3) (emphasis added)

The battlefield is the mind.

Too many Christians and too many churches get the order wrong. We talk about right living, right choices, godly behavior, and holiness of life. All those things are true, and so important. As a pastor/author, I have written two books about holiness and sanctification, so I'll say I'm second to none in that emphasis.

But how do we get there? How do we get to right living?

I'll start by saying you can't get to right living by preaching right living.

The reason is because right believing produces right living. We have to teach and preach for right believing. Right thinking produces right believing. Right doctrine produces right believing. Here's the pattern: Right doctrine > Right believing > Right living. Get it?

So when the devil comes in, he's working way less on the *living* level and way more on the doctrine and thinking level. Paul warns, "Beware lest anyone take you captive through philosophy and empty deceit, according to the tradition of men, according to the basic principles of the world, and not according to Christ" (Colossians 2:8).

I encourage you to buy a really nice Bible—preferably the same translation your pastor uses for preaching. Ask which one if you don't know. If your pastor doesn't have a preferred translation, then go with the New King James or the New American Standard Bible.

Also, bring it to church. Open it up when your pastor preaches. Bring a pencil and make notes in it.

A digital Bible is okay too. But you should still have a nice Bible that you can wear out and grow old with.

Bring your Sword to Church! The devil hates that!

Your mind is a battlefield.

2. SWORD - Your primary weapon against doctrines of demons are the doctrines of the Word of God.

The sword of the Spirit is the Word of God.

The Holy Spirit has proclaimed war, and he wields a two-edged sword. The Word of God is that sword.

It is the Spirit's sword because:

- The Holy Spirit inspired the Bible, so that every line is the utterance of God, perfect and without error in every word and truth.
- The Holy Spirit illuminates the Bible, so that any person hearing or reading or studying can understand what God has said.
- The Holy Spirit applies the Bible, so that when the Word gets in you, the lies you believe are surgically removed and you actually begin to think God's thoughts after him.

It is the great mission of the church, of its leaders, and of all the people of God to teach, communicate, preach, and proclaim the doctrines of the Word of God.

The supreme message of the Holy Spirt is to glorify Jesus Christ. The Holy Spirit does not glorify himself. The message of the church is not to be Holy Spirit, Holy Spirit, Holy Spirit.

Jesus said, "But when the Helper comes, whom I shall send to you from the Father, the Spirit of truth who proceeds from the Father, He will testify of Me" (John 15:26). That is what the Spirit has done, is doing, and will do. He bears witness to Christ.

In fact the whole Bible is in some way pointing to Jesus. In theology, this is called Christology, the doctrine of Christ, which is organized into two great parts:

- Part One: the Person of Christ.
- Part Two: the Work of Christ.

After the resurrection, Jesus was making many appearances in different places to different believers. In one of those appearances, Jesus catches up to two men walking on a road from Jerusalem to a city called Emmaus. He overhears their conversation. They are talking about Jesus, and about reports of his resurrection. And Jesus can also hear that they are both very, very confused and very, very sad.

> "So it was, while they conversed and reasoned, that Jesus Himself drew near and went with them. But their eyes were restrained, so that they did not know Him. And He said to them, 'What kind of conversation is this that you have with one another as you walk and are sad?'" (Luke 24:15-17)

They don't recognize Jesus, and they say, "Have you been hiding under a rock? Everybody knows this stuff. Jesus was a mighty prophet. He was horribly crucified. He died. And this is the third day, and now we're hearing these rumors that he is risen again. And these rumors have been confirmed by reliable eyewitnesses. And we don't know what to think!"

> "Then He said to them, 'O foolish ones, and slow of heart to believe in all that the prophets have spoken! Ought not the Christ [=the Messiah, Jesus] to have suffered these things and to enter into His glory?' And beginning at Moses and all the Prophets, He expounded [interpreted] to them in all the Scriptures the things concerning Himself." (Luke 24:25-27)

Moses and the Prophets are the whole Old Testament, the whole Bible as it existed in that day. The New Testament wasn't written yet, but it had the same theme.

That theme was Christ. If they hadn't been foolish and slow of heart, they would have found right there in their Bibles everything they needed to know.

That from the beginning, God promised a coming Savior. He would be their Messiah and their King. But first he would suffer and shed his blood and die to reconcile sinners to God. Then he would rise again.

With two men on the Road to Emmaus, Jesus gives the best

Bible study ever experienced on planet earth. I hope in heaven I can see the video of this Bible study.

The whole Bible speaks of Christ. All the prophecies, the sacrifices, the offerings, the priesthood, the garments, the vessels of the tabernacle. All the promises, all the moral law, all the explications of it. All the denunciations of sin. All the requirements of perfection. In symbols, in illustrations, in parables, and in plain teaching, all of Scripture—which is inspired word for word by the Holy Spirit—speaks of Christ.

So we say:

> *The heart of Scripture is Christ.*
> *The heart of Christ is Grace.*
> *And the heart of Grace is the Cross.*

This is the explicit mission of the Holy Spirit; Jesus said, "He will testify of me." He's been doing it since the dawn of creation. He's been doing it since he inspired the 40-plus authors of Scripture. He's been doing that in every communication and instruction ever given on earth that in any way is true to the Word of God.

It's all about Jesus.

Because when you assemble all the doctrines of the Word of God, you get a profile of Jesus Christ in his person and work.

Why does this matter?

Because when you get Christology right—the Person of Christ in his human and divine natures, plus the Work of Christ, centered on his Cross, and culminating in his glorious return and millennial reign—you get the grace of God unleashed psychologically in your soul.

> **WHEN YOU GET JESUS RIGHT THEOLOGICALLY IN YOUR MIND, YOU GET THE GRACE OF GOD UNLEASHED PSYCHOLOGICALLY IN YOUR SOUL.**

The most destructive force in your life are the lies you believe, taught to you by Satan, coupled with the labels of doom he has slapped on you, taught to you by this insane culture. So that the most life-giving force in your life will be the truth of Jesus Christ and his Cross and the riches of his grace for you.

"For you know the grace of our Lord Jesus Christ, that though He was rich, yet for your sakes He became poor, that you through His poverty might become rich." (2 Corinthians 8:9)

Jesus Christ is the answer to your poverty in every way shape and form.

Jesus is your victory.

Jesus is your destiny.

Jesus is your majesty.

Jesus is your glory.

The greatest tragedy, and the greatest opening we give to the devil, is to be foolish and slow of heart to believe in all that the prophets have spoken of him, being moved by the Holy Spirit.

If the Sword of the Spirit is the Word of God, then biblical illiteracy is the Church surrendering its arms.

I know that sounds harsh, and I know that's bad news, and you know I want to be the bearer of good news.

But if the grace of God is there for us, and we don't take it, then I'm going to write, preach, teach, motivate, and, well, nag you until you do.

So here's some good news.

3. HEARING - The secret of growing both knowledge and faith is by hearing again and again the teachings of God's amazing grace.

This is not a complicated thing.

I have said that the way to put on each piece of armor is by faith.

But what if your faith is small? What if your faith is weak? What should you do? Scripture answers: "So then faith comes by hearing, and hearing by the word of Christ." (Romans 10:17) The ESV, NASB, NIV, NLT, and all modern translations say *Christ* rather than *God*—I have discussed this earlier.

What you are doing right now is how you put muscle on your faith. Hearing or reading the Word of Christ. Learning of his grace. Being reminded of his love. Making the case why your salvation is real. Understanding why the devil is a liar, and why his accusations can't stick to you. Taking in the good news of why guilt can't dominate you. Learning how your sins are paid for and that you've been redeemed. Understanding you are set free and your dominion is restored. I could go on.

We are supposed to learn the whole counsel of God in such a way that we can trace all these powerful salvation-blessings back to Christ.

The Word of Christ—the teaching of grace, the explanation and explication of a covenant of mercy between God and his people—is the secret weapon of making your faith strong.

There's a popular website where a popular church leader suggested that when you study the Bible, you should ask five questions:

1. Is there a command to obey?
2. Is there an example to follow?
3. Is there a promise to claim?
4. Is there a sin to avoid?
5. Is there a principle to follow?

This is exactly the problem with us Christians. Law, law, grace, law, law, grace. Eighty percent law, twenty percent grace. May I humbly propose five different questions to guide your study of God's Word:

1. How is God's love taught here?
2. How is saving grace deepened?
3. How is Christ glorified in his Person and his Work?
4. How are my riches and privileges in Christ expanded?
5. How is God shown to be a better Father to me than I've ever thought before?

Look for that. Study for that. This is what preaching should be, and this is what Bible study should focus on. Because faith comes by hearing and hearing by the Word of Christ. Because this is what Jesus did on the Road to Emmaus, and this is the pattern for all the ages since then.

When Jesus and those two believers finally reached Emmaus, they sat together and dined together. He broke bread with them and hung out for a while, and then we get this:

> "Now it came to pass, as He sat at the table with them, that He took bread, blessed and broke it, and gave it to them. Then their eyes were opened and they knew Him; and He vanished from their sight. And they said to one another, 'Did not our heart burn within us while He talked with us on the road, and while He opened the Scriptures to us?'" (Luke 24:30-32)

The truth had an *emotional* effect on them—*their hearts were burning*. That's what the Word of God does when its communicated to point to grace. When you keep on hearing the Word of grace, your faith grows strong. When you starve yourself of the Word of grace, your faith grows weak.

I hope and pray that wherever you go, and wherever God may direct your path, that you never forsake the gathering of saints called *church*, and that you attach yourself faithfully to a church that proclaims Jesus Christ, Calvary's Love, and God's amazing grace.

4. ACTIVATION - You activate the Sword of the Spirit by speaking the truth of God's grace and provision into every trial you face.

Here's what I mean. When Paul explains the Sword of the Spirit as the Word of God, he does not use the normal Greek word for *Word*. The normal Greek word is *logos*. It can mean word, or message, or truth.

But this word isn't *logos*, it's *rhema* (ray-mah).

Our charismatic friends will tell you that *rhema* means a fresh word that the Holy Spirit invents for you when you need help. I cannot, however, find that view supported by credible scholarship in New Testament Greek.

Rhema just means to speak out, or say, or express the Word of God and the truth of grace. Say it. Say it from the heart. Speak forth God's Word, especially as it communicates the wonderful Covenant of Grace, the victory of Christ, and the Cross of our Salvation. Declare it from your heart. That's the idea.

Do you know what the devil does when you hit him with a so-called "fresh word" of the Spirit? He laughs at you. It's a plastic sword.

But do you know what the devil does when you hit him with an expression of the truth of the Word of God? He runs from you. It's the finest steel blade of the Sword of the Spirit.

You wield the sword by saying God's truth, by speaking God's Word, by declaring God's grace.

When the devil tempted Jesus, do you remember what Jesus said?

Each time, Jesus said, It is written. It is written. It is written. He quoted Scripture every times (Matthew 4:4-7). The devil had to retreat.

Jesus wielded the Sword of the Spirit by *speaking* God's grace and provision in the face of the Evil One's attack.

When Goliath taunted David, David declared,

"You come to me with a sword, with a spear, and with a javelin. But I come to you in the name of the LORD of hosts, the God of the armies of Israel, whom you have defied. This day the LORD will deliver you into my hand... Then all this assembly shall know that the LORD does not save with sword and spear; for the battle is the LORD's, and He will give you into our hands." (1 Samuel 17:45-47)

He didn't exactly quote Scripture, but he didn't have to. Every word he spoke is filled with grace and truth. He jabbed that Sword of the Spirit right into the head of that giant, and the giant came tumbling down. Your giants will too, because the weapons of our warfare are mighty through God. The Sword of the Spirit is the saying forth of the Word of God.

When the demonized King Nebuchadnezzar threatened Shadrach, Meschech, and Abednego with the furnace of roaring fire, commanding, "Worship me or burn!" they said, "Our God whom we serve is able to deliver us from the burning fiery furnace, and He will deliver us from your hand, O king. But if not, let it be known to you, O king, that we do not serve your gods, nor will we worship the gold image which you have set up.'" (Daniel 3:17-18)

They spoke the power of God into the situation, and God walked with them through the fire. They were wielding the Sword of the Spirit which is the Word of God.

If you have the Word of God in your heart, you have the invincible power of God at your fingertips.

Speak truth into every situation. Speak power. Speak love. Speak grace. Speak the promises of God. Speak hope. Speak the blood of Christ. Speak resurrection power. Speak life from the dead. Speak abundance. Speak healing. Speak blessing. Speak better things. Speak the name of God. Speak the presence of God. Speak the character of God. Speak courage. Speak power. Speak freedom. Speak success. Speak abundance. Speak victory.

Speak truth, theology, Scripture, doctrine.

Speak it, say it, sing it, pray it, shout it.

Soldier of Christ, Speak Jesus!

Unsheath the Sword of the Spirit and call forth the Word of God.

Because, if you will for one shining moment, declare that the Battle is the Lord's, and tell evil you will not bow, and say to the Tempter, It is written, It is written, It is written!

Or if you will simply claim that epic promise, Behold I am with you always, even to the ends of the earth, then one day—it might be here, there, or in the air—you will find out that when you wielded the Sword of the Spirit, God sent a hundred tall angels, clothed with light, with swords in their hands to surround you and to send the devil and the demons back to the darkness where they belong.

The Word of God is living and powerful, even when you are not.

So speak it into your depression, speak it into your heartbreak, speak it into your illness, speak it into your debt, speak it into your addiction and loneliness and bitterness and despair—and all of heaven will rush to your aid, because the child of God, clothed in the armor of Christ, can never, ever fail.

REFLECTION AND DISCUSSION

1. How do you feel after reading the missionaries' story at the beginning of this chapter?
2. Do you go to a church where the messages come from the Bible? Why does this matter in spiritual warfare?
3. How was David swinging the Sword of the Spirit even though he wasn't quoting Bible verses when he dispatched Goliath? What does that teach you?

4. How knowledgable are you about basic Bible doctrine? How important do you think doctrine is? How important is it to other believers you know?
5. What are some qualities and abilities of your Sword identified in Hebrews 4:12?

NOTE: if you would like to strengthen your Sword by learning some basic Bible doctrine, I have written a book called *Know What You Believe*. You can find it here on Amazon: https://amzn.to/45nNOy7

CHAPTER 14
THE SWORD OF THE SPIRIT, PART 2

Satan comes as a serpent in the persons of false teachers, and by them labours to put a cheat on us, and cozen us with error for truth.
~William Gurnall

DOMINION

IF I COULD DISTILL the central issue of spiritual warfare into one word, it would be *dominion*. We have already discussed dominion in several chapters, but here, I'd like to take an even deeper dive into the subject.

1. OUR OBJECTIVE: Every Christian is a warrior in a cosmic battle to get back one primary thing: your God-given DOMINION.

In the Garden of Eden, God gave Adam and Eve dominion. Dominion means the right to rule. It means the power and the authority to rule the realm of your life. It means freedom. It means the complete absence of domination.

No addiction, dysfunction, depression, anxiety, PTSD (because no T, trauma), poverty, conflict, sorrow, sadness, or pain.

The realm over which Adam and Eve enjoyed dominion was the Paradise of God, the Garden of Eden, the vast realm of beauty, pleasure, goodness, love, and peace.

It was safe there. They held the scepter of the realm, and no sorrows intruded into it at all.

We have no idea how long this lasted, until it all collapsed in a burning heap of smoldering rubble on one terrible, horrible, no good, very bad day—a day of catastrophe and ruin—the day that, in theology, is called the Fall.

If you know the story, you know Satan egged them on. Satan questioned God's Word. He tempted Eve. Eve tempted Adam. They sinned, the devil laughed, the demons cackled, the angels watched, God handed down righteous curses on the whole created realm, and in one hideous moment, this beautiful, lush, gorgeous world was utterly ruined.

That is why this fallen world is a morally-broken Pain Machine. Paul explains, "For if by the one man's offense death reigned through the one…" (Romans 5:17).

The one man is Adam. When sin galloped into the world, death came riding on its back. In that moment, the human race was broken and corrupted. In that moment, by one man's disobedience, the whole race was made sinners (Romans 5:19). The single worst and most consequential part of the entire disaster is this:

2. DEFEAT: When sin entered the human race, the scepter of dominion was transferred from mankind to Satan.

This fallen realm is the devil's. The kingdoms of earth are his. In the temptations of Jesus, the devil offered Jesus all the kingdoms of the world and their glory. He could offer those things because he reigns over those things.

Three times, Jesus called him the Ruler of this World (John 12:31).

Paul called him the God of this age (2 Corinthians 4:4).

The whole world-system lies under his sway, says the Bible, because the whole world-system is his (1 John 5:19).

So the devil influences all the systems of the world — music, arts, education, media, culture, government, even religion — the devil is constantly reinforcing a philosophy that cements his dominion over our world.

3. SATAN'S OBJECTIVE: In this great cosmic conflict of the ages, the devil's grand objective is the moral and psychological entrapment of humans.

Rewind in time back to the days of Daniel the prophet, about six hundred years before Christ. The world at that time was under the boot of the Babylonian Empire. The king was a psychopath named Nebuchadnezzar, who worshipped demonic deities and made himself a deity.

When he destroyed Jerusalem and enslaved the Jews, King Nebuchadnezzar kidnapped four teenagers and brought them to Babylon for brainwashing. Their names were Daniel, Hananiah, Mishael, and Azariah. You might know the last three as Shadrach, Meshech, and Abednego—but those were Babylonian names the king gave them as part of their indoctrination.

> "Then the king instructed Ashpenaz, the master of his eunuchs, to bring some of the children of Israel and some of the king's descendants and some of the nobles, young men in whom there was no blemish, but good-looking, gifted in all wisdom, possessing knowledge and quick to understand, who had ability to serve in the

king's palace, and whom they might teach the language and literature of the Chaldeans." (Daniel 1:3-4)

That's fine, right? The literature and language of the Chaldeans (Babylonians), that's harmless, right? Well it's not harmless because their literature and language was saturated with idol worship, and the Jews knew that idols are demons in disguise. Even their meals were, let's just say, not what Jews should eat.

But they were well treated. They were even given the royal cafeteria. But don't you know that well-treated captives are still captives and well-treated slaves are still slaves. Captives can be brainwashed into making captivity their new normal.

This is the devil's plan for your life.

In this great cosmic conflict of the ages, the devil's grand objective is the moral and psychological entrapment of us humans.

If he can't put chains on your wrists, he'll put them on your heart.

- "And that they may come to their senses and escape the snare of the devil, having been taken captive by him to do his will." (2 Timothy 2:26)
- "While they promise them liberty, they themselves are slaves of corruption; for by whom a person is overcome, by him also he is brought into bondage." (2 Peter 2:19)
- "[Jesus became human so that] through death He might destroy him who had the power of death, that is, the devil, and release those who through fear of death were all their lifetime subject to bondage." (Hebrews 2:14-15)

Notice the precise wording: Bondage. Overcome. Slaves. Snare. Taken captive. All of this is subjugation. All of this is the Enemy of Our Souls, smiling and laughing as he luxuriates in his stolen dominion over the souls of this fallen world.

Because of the Fall, the power of Satan was now greater than the combined might of the whole human race. We could not break his chains. We could not end his dominion. Only a greater power could set us free.

That greater power is the Person of Our Lord Jesus Christ.

The power by which he vaporized the chains and prison bars Satan had forged, and the power by which Jesus broke the devil's hypnotic trance was not the power of overwhelming force but of substitutionary death: "[Jesus became human so that] through death He might destroy him who had the power of death, that is, the devil, and release those who through fear of death were all their lifetime subject to bondage." (Hebrews 2:14-15)

The satanic reign of terror is finished in Jesus Christ crucified and risen again.

> THE SATANIC REIGN OF TERROR IS FINISHED IN JESUS CHRIST CRUCIFIED AND RISEN AGAIN.

All your lifetime, you've been subject to bondage. All your lifetime, you've been Shadrach, Meshech, and Abednego in some variation—captured by alien forces, and being persuaded to make captivity your new normal.

But you've been released. You've been set free. You've been redeemed by the blood of the Lamb.

4. VICTORY: On the day of your salvation, you got your dominion back.

Come hell or high water, you got your dominion back. I am not making this up: "For if by the one man's offense death reigned through the one, much more those who receive abundance of grace and of the gift of righteousness will reign in life through the One, Jesus Christ." (Romans 5:17)

One man's sin, Adam, was enough to plunge the world into the reign of death.

One man's Person and Work, Jesus, is enough to elevate every believer in Jesus back to the throne of your own soul and enable you to reign in life.

You get your dominion back. You reign. You rule. You reign in life. You've received not just grace but the abundance of grace. You've received the gift of righteousness, and that means you "reign in life."

Jesus grasped the scepter from the gnarly hand of Satan, washed it in his blood, and gave it back to you. This is the victory and the triumph and the glory of our salvation. That's a fact. That's a truth. That's a reality. That's what salvation does for you.

Aren't you glad you're saved? Aren't you thankful for Jesus?

Now this is all Christian theology. It is the theology of salvation, called Soteriology, coupled with the theology of human nature, called Biblical Anthropology.

But there is a massive disconnect going on.

5. STRUGGLE: Our new struggle is to forge a link between the *theology* of our dominion and the *psychology* of our souls.

This is the massive problem that made me write this book. This is the missing link.

I am saying that the missing link is the Armor of God.

God put this armor in the Bible because the devil has not given up on you. He lost his throne, yes. He lost his crown. He lost his scepter and his dominion.

But the devil still has his wiles. He's still a roaring lion. He's still spewing doctrines of demons across the sidewalk of your life. You have to step around it every single day. He's still brainwashing, still mind-controlling, and still coming alongside you as an angel of light.

The devil has lost his bite but still has his bark. He's still barking orders at you like he's still in charge. But he's not in charge. You are in charge, reigning in life, under the Lordship of Christ.

But what does that matter if your soul still jumps at his commands and bites at his shiny allurements?

What does it matter if the devil's psychological operations are in full force and most Christians clip along blissfully unaware?

6. NEED: You, Christian, have been set free, but your soul still needs rehab.

Satan, sin, hell, fear, addiction, temptation, anxiety, anger, your past, the horoscope, predisposition, trauma, victimhood, failure, uncertainty, debt, depression, and fear of death—why do these forces still dominate Christians who've been set free from domination?

What's going on?

What's going on is that God says to put on your armor, and within that, he says to take up the Sword of the Spirit, and most Christians don't do either.

Most Christians don't know the Bible in depth, and most churches don't really teach the Bible in depth. Generally, when they do, it's overwhelmingly legalistic.

That's why most believers limp beneath their troubles rather than mount up with wings like eagles. They have the Spirit, because they're saved. But they don't have the Sword. Any Christian who lays down their sword is disarmed against the wiles of the devil.

But that doesn't have to be you.

I lovingly exhort you to take up the Sword of the Spirit which is the Word of God, because by that Word you will slay the strongholds of deceit still rooted in your own soul, that war against your dominion.

BACK TO BABYLON

The psychotic king grows in power and glory year after year. He is the mightiest king on earth. He becomes grandiose in his thinking.

The king builds a massive statue of gold. It's a 90-foot tall image of himself. There it stands, glistening both in the sunlight as well as in the light of the blazing furnace he has built to spotlight his own majesty and glory.

He sends out messengers to all the nations of the empire, commanding all the rulers of all the kingdoms of the known world to come. They will gather before his golden image. They will bow or they will burn.

Picture the scene, there in the vast flatlands called Shinar. Teeming multitudes of dignitaries from all the earth are there in their robes and turbans, some in crowns. A hot sun blazes down on food vendors and booths. It's a carnival atmosphere; the king has spared no expense. You can almost hear the cacophony of the crowds over the roar of the furnace of fire.

The military might of Babylon stands ready to enforce the king's decree.

The golden idol, visible from miles away, shines with the radiance of the all glorious King Nebuchadnezzar.

Next to it sits the royal orchestra, with horns and strings and choirs.

It is one of the greatest displays of the world's pomp in all of human history. It is the *cosmos diabolicus*—the devil's world—at its best on full display.

The time has come. The king's heralds decree that when the orchestra plays, all the rulers of earth will bow and worship the king's image.

The king processes to his elevated throne. The cue is given. The orchestra plays. All across the plain, kings and queens, magi and wise men, judges and governors, treasurers and dignitaries drop to their knees and bury their faces in the dirt to worship the king.

What would you have done?

Everyone. Everyone. Everyone bows.

Thousands and thousands kiss the dirt. Thousands and thousands worship the self-deified king, an ambassador of Satan, and preview of the Antichrist.

Everyone bows.

Except…

… we'll come back to this.

7. WEAPONS: The strongest weapon to rehab your soul is by hearing *and saying* the truth of God's grace into every situation you face.

Do you know who your number one audience is? Do you know who is always listening to the words you say? Don't say God. Don't say angels. Don't say demons. That's all true.

But the deepest truth is that *your own soul* is listening to the words you say all day long, all life long.

Your tender heart is a captive audience.

What messages are you preaching to your own heart?

What neural pathways are you reinforcing by your words?

If you have made your mouth a conduit for defeat, you will be defeated. If you have made your mouth a conduit for messages of victimization, you will define yourself as a victim. You will be stuck in a prison with the doors wide open.

If you have made your mouth a continual stream of fear and loathing, your whole psychological state will bow and kiss the dirt before the idols you have made.

You will join the ranks of thousands and thousands of men and women who should be rulers, but are bowing to the dominion of a psychopath.

You will do this *because* your pronouncements are out of alignment with the Word of God.

To speak words of bitterness, anger, hatred, self-pity, or defeat about yourself is to create self-fulfilling prophecies in your own heart. To speak toxic words is to shape a toxic psychology. Your heart is listening. If you keep telling yourself words of bondage, you will condition yourself back into the same emotional subjugation that Jesus died to free you from.

By your graceless words, you keep killing your dominion (Matthew 12:37).

You can bow to any king you choose. Some choose fentanyl, alcohol, pornography, debt, bad luck, rage, bitterness, grandiosity, materialism, money, sex, power, philanthropy, authority, comfort, pleasure, or the betterment of all mankind. Some choose Nebuchadnezzar. All of these rulers are the devil in disguise. Make no mistake, these rulers will steal your dominion in a heartbeat.

When Nebuchadnezzar's orchestra played and when thousands bowed and kissed the earth, there were three men standing.

Three men who said, I'm not going to bow to your idols. No.

Oh what a scene the king created! He lost it. He was furious, spitting mad, out of control.

He sent his guards to drag Shadrach, Mechech, and Abednego before him. He was shocked when he saw them, because he knew them. He respected them.

But he couldn't lose face, and he gave them one more chance.

Watch how three teenagers in a life or death situation boldly wield the Sword of the Spirit.

When the demonized King Nebuchadnezzar threatened them with the furnace of roaring fire, commanding, "Worship me or burn!"

They said:

"Our God whom we serve is able to deliver us from the burning fiery furnace, and He will deliver us from your hand, O king. But if not, let it be known to you, O king, that we do not serve your gods, nor will we worship the gold image which you have set up." (Daniel 3:17-18)

They spoke the truth of God's omnipotent grace into the situation, and God walked with them through the fire. They can imprison your body; they can destroy your body; but they cannot touch your soul, and they cannot diminish your rewards in heaven.

These men of faith wielded the Sword of the Spirit which is the Word of God. The devil couldn't touch them. And not even the mightiest king with the mightiest armies on earth held dominion over them.

They were masters of their fate and of their realm, because they spoke the Sword of the Spirit which is the Word of God.

This is spiritual warfare at its finest.

The strongest way to rehab your soul is by hearing *and saying* the truth of God's grace into every situation you face.

SAY IT...

I am the righteousness of God in Christ.

No weapon formed against me shall prosper.

In all these things, I am more than a conqueror.

You come to me with a sword and a spear, but I come to you in the name of the Lord of Hosts.

The Battle is the Lord's.

God causes all things to work together for good.

Faith is the victory.

Jesus loves me, this I know, for the Bible tells me so.

Nothing shall separate me from the Love of God.

I am secure forever.

I am saved, and I can never lose it.

I am forgiven.

I am redeemed.

I am blessed.

I am beloved.

I am a child of Love.

It's going to be okay.

I have a destiny.

I have provision.

I have protection.

I have abundance.

I have grace because…

I have Jesus.

Say it. Utter it. Mutter it. Mumble it. Shout it. Pray it. Sing it.

There is one King in all Creation who needs nothing from you. He will take nothing and give everything. He will bless. He will provide.

His greatest delight is to see you filled with the abundance of grace, standing in his gift of righteousness, and rising to your full stature as a child of heaven, reigning in life because Jesus won your dominion back.

Preach that sermon to your heart a dozen times a day, and you will reign in life, and the devil will flee from you.

REFLECTION AND DISCUSSION

1. Why do you think the devil has always been after our dominion?
2. What are some of the most powerful ways the devil uses today to entrap people? In what ways do you see this happening among people you know?
3. Explain in your own words how the Armor of God is the missing link between theology and psychology.
4. In what ways did Shadrach, Meshech, and Abednego speak the Sword of the Spirit into their great moment of spiritual battle?
5. What does Revelation 12:15 tell you about the power of the Word of Christ?

CHAPTER 15
THE PROFILE OF A CHAMPION

You now have, Christian, the armour of God; but take heed thou forgettest not to engage the God of this armour by humble prayer for your assistance, lest for all this you be worsted in the fight.
~William Gurnall

THE MAIN THING

THE MAIN PURPOSE of the Church is to create a certain kind of person. It is first of all, the kind of person who has become a believer in Jesus. Then it is the kind of Christian who has become the person described in Paul's epic description of the warfare we are in:

> "Put on the whole armor of God, that you may be able to stand against the wiles of the devil. For we do not wrestle against flesh and blood, but against principalities, against powers, against the rulers of the darkness of this age, against spiritual hosts of wickedness in the heavenly places. Therefore take up the whole armor of

God, that you may be able to withstand in the evil day, and having done all, to stand." (Ephesians 6:11-13)

The purpose of the Church, a church, and any ministry worth anything, is to equip you, mold you, and motivate you so that you may be able to withstand the devil in the evil day, and having done all, to stand. Stand in wholeness. Stand in grace. Stand for Christ and the Gospel. Every church worthy of the name church has that as its mission. That is mission of my church. That is the constitution for the Church at large, the body of Christ in the world.

Any church not working to create that kind of Christian is not following the will of God.

We are commissioned by God to create a certain kind of Christian that we might fulfill a specific divine purpose.

THE PROFILE OF A CHAMPION

"...[P]raying always with all prayer and supplication in the Spirit, being watchful to this end with all perseverance and supplication for all the saints—" (Ephesians 6:18)

Paul wraps up the Armor of God with prayer, because prayer is the weapon that makes every other weapon work. Prayer is the toggle switch. Prayer is how we put on our armor. This armor, activated by prayer, is *how* you become the Christian who stands.

The devil has not laid down his arms. The warfare has not ceased, and it will not cease until Jesus returns. God wants you to stand in victory.

Elsewhere in the Bible, St. Peter expresses the same idea when he writes, "[That you may become] children of God without fault in the midst of a crooked and perverse generation, among whom you shine as lights in the world" (Philippians 2:15).

God has an agenda for your life. He's written a mission statement for you. Let's break it down into eight qualities.

EIGHT QUALITIES

1. MISSION: Your mission is to become a Champion of Grace and Truth in a culture of pain and confusion.

The world needs you. Your friends need you. Your neighbors. Your teammates. Your family. They are trapped in a crooked and perverse generation.

There is so much sadness. So much confusion and pain. So God commissions us, just like he commissioned Jesus, to go out into a crooked and perverse generation to shine as lights in the world. Jesus said, "As the Father has sent me, I also send you" (John 20:21).

Now it's our turn. Let's become Champions of grace and truth in a culture of confusion and pain.

That sounds like a very tall order, and it is. It's a high calling. It's a hard thing. Actually, humanly speaking, it's an impossible thing… were it not for the amazing truth that the things that are impossible for us are possible with God.

You can actually become the kind of person that God wants you to be. This high calling is well within reach of every child of God.

Why is the world falling apart all around us? Why is culture in such disarray? Why the chaos? Why the ascendancy of evil? Why the destruction of the family, the failure of marriage, and why so much trauma to children?

Could it be because so very few believers are fulfilling their mission? We have laid aside our armor. We have forgotten our battle. We have been distracted by so many other things.

It's time for the church to be the Church. Soldier of Christ arise! Let's go! From this time forward, put your life on a path of spiritual growth and accept your mission as a soldier of the Cross. That's my prayer for you. That's my exhortation. That's why I wrote this book.

Nothing will get better in our society until we Christians turn back to Christ with our whole hearts.

> "If My people who are called by My name will humble themselves, and pray and seek My face, and turn from their wicked ways, then I will hear from heaven, and will forgive their sin and heal their land." (2 Chronicles 7:14)

2. STRENGTH - A Champion of Grace and Truth finds their strength in the Lord and in the power of His might.

Human power can never accomplish the will of God. Only divine power — God's power — can do that. This is the whole point of the Armor of God. The weapons of our warfare are mighty through God. It's grace, not works. It's faith, not striving. It's God not us.

I want to bring us back to an episode in the life of Jesus to make this three dimensional and real. We looked at this same story back in chapter 11. There, we used Matthew's account of the event. Here, let's use Mark's account. In chapter 11, I said there was a powerful and beautiful secret hiding in plain sight.

> "Then one of the crowd answered and said, 'Teacher, I brought You my son, who has a mute spirit. And wherever it seizes him, it throws him down; he foams at the mouth, gnashes his teeth, and becomes rigid. So I spoke to Your disciples, that they should cast it out, but they could not.'" (Mark 9:17-18)

Never underestimate how much the devil hates you. This is not a game. It's called spiritual warfare for a reason.

Here is this poor boy, suffering horribly. So the heartbroken father brings him to the disciples of Jesus, but they could not deliver him from the power of the dark side. How does Jesus respond?

> "He answered him and said, 'O faithless generation, how long shall I be with you? How long shall I bear with you? Bring him to Me.'" (Mark 9:19)

The emotion in the words of Jesus is not primarily anger; it is a pathos-filled expression of the infinite pain Jesus felt over mankind's unbelief. This is personal sorrow to the max.

What triggers this exclamation from Jesus can be summed up in one word: Empathy.

3. EMPATHY - A Champion of Grace and Truth feels heartfelt empathy for the pains of a lost and dying world.

O Lord, give us tender hearts. O Lord, burden our souls with the same care Jesus felt for lost people trapped outside the streams of grace.

Jesus grieves the pains of this man and his boy. He grieves the pains of the world. He is saddened even more because it doesn't have to be this way.

His generation is so unreceptive to the healing streams of grace that could be theirs. They are unreceptive to the good news of a full atonement for sin, to the victorious proclamation of a decisive defeat of the devil, and to the rich and glorious birthright that is theirs in Jesus Christ. They are unreceptive to a covenant of grace to displace their worn out covenant of works. So this generation wallows in needless confusion and needless pain.

It's just so sad.

This was the Jesus Generation. No surprise, but it's our generation too. So many are disinterested and unreceptive to anything having to do with Jesus and his salvation.

So here is this aching, heartbroken father whose son is suffering horribly at the hands of Satan, and Jesus aches for him.

But it's another layer sadder for Jesus because his own disciples failed. They failed this father, his tormented son, and they failed Jesus.

The man brought his son to them, and the demon beat them. The Pain Machine won. They tried. They failed. They moved on. Sorry. The boy with the demon remains the boy with the demon, that's just too bad.

But Jesus knew it's not supposed to be that way. He's the one who said, "...I will build My church, and the gates of Hell shall not prevail against it" (Matthew 16:18).

But in this case, the gates of hell *did* prevail.

Now, here's the kicker. If you back up to the scene right before this scene, you see Jesus taking his core disciples to school.

There is an event called the Transfiguration. In that event, for one shining moment, God lifts the veil that hides the true glory of Jesus. God the Father lets a few disciples glimpse the true glory of Christ for one brief moment, and it is awesome.

Jesus blazes forth like a thousand suns. He shines with majesty and power and glory and so much that he takes the disciples' breath away. They fall to the ground. For this one moment, they see Jesus as heaven sees him, as the angels see him, and as the demons see him. He is transfigured before their eyes. He is glorious. Frightening. Majestic. Buzzing with power and blazing with light. It's the experience of a lifetime.

Suddenly, it's over. The Transfiguration glory switches off.

This was a message to these disciples. This was a revelation to them. This was a giant shout from heaven of the majesty and the victory of the King of kings and Lord of lords.

Can you imagine if later today God reached down to you, and carried you up to heaven. He lets you see Jesus, unveiled, on the throne of glory for just sixty seconds. You see mighty angels flying and worshiping, streets glistening with gold, the paradise of God.

You see innumerable masses of saints of ages past, now glorified and singing his praise and reigning with him. You see the Lord Jesus, shining in his blinding radiance, ruling and dispatching orders to angels to answer prayers and shepherd the universe.

If you could stand there and just watch him for one minute, and then come back to earth and live out your days, would you ever be the same again?

No way. That would change you forever.

That's exactly the experience the disciples had.

And the very next thing is that a man brings his demon-afflicted boy to the disciples, and they try to deliver him, they can't, *and they give up.* "Sorry, sir. Who's next?"

> "He answered him and said, 'O faithless generation, how long shall I be with you? How long shall I bear with you? Bring him to Me.'" (Mark 9:19)

Jesus asks how long he has to stay with them. How long he has to bear with them. Why does he ask *how long?*

Jesus is stuck here until they get their act together, that's why.

Jesus could not go away until he had left these disciples strong enough to stand by themselves and strong enough to lay the foundations of the church.

He couldn't leave until *they* were ready.

So he gave them a giant boost with a vision of his triumph and strength.

4. VISION - A Champion of Grace and Truth will stand strong in the never-fading vision of Christ's majesty, glory, and strength.

The church is triumphant when we see Jesus triumphant.

Christians are triumphant when we see Jesus triumphant.

Why did the disciples fail?

They forgot Christ's triumph and strength. They forgot the

vision of the Transfiguration. They barked at a demon, and the demon barked back, and they ran away like sissies. They quit on this kid.

When that happened, they should have known a secret technique. We've already seen that secret technique in this text. I wonder if you caught it yet. You might have.

But we'll save it for now.

"Then they brought him to Him. And when he saw Him, immediately the spirit convulsed him, and he fell on the ground and wallowed, foaming at the mouth. So He asked his father, 'How long has this been happening to him?' And he said, 'From childhood. And often he has thrown him both into the fire and into the water to destroy him. But if You can do anything, have compassion on us and help us.'" (Mark 9:20-22)

Satan is an abuser. He is the evil step-father of all abuse. The sheer savagery of this bloodthirsty devil is beyond comprehension. Look at what he's doing to this boy.

But we know that the devil's doom is sure. We know that the God of peace will crush Satan under our feet shortly (Romans 16:20).

Notice what the father says and then what Jesus says.

The father says, "If you can do anything..."

Jesus brushes that off. He knows he can do anything. He knows divine omnipotence is at his fingertips.

It's not if *he* can do anything. The only "if" is this one: "Jesus said to him, 'If you can believe, all things are possible to him who believes.'" (Mark 9:23)

Not *if he*, but *if you!*

That's always the case. It's never "if God!" It's always "if you!"

If you can believe.

Jesus says, don't ask if I can, ask if you can.

Because if your faith lays hold on God's omnipotence, all things are possible to you. Notice, this isn't saying that you can do all conceivable things, like flying or turning invisible or turning your enemy into a frog; that's not the promise.

The promise is that you can get all things, and receive all things that the promises of God are blessing you with.

It is incredible to think that this Jewish peasant named Jesus should plant himself in front of the human race—

That he could stare in the face the burdened sinful race of humankind, call all people to himself, and pledge Himself—

- Come to me and I will cleanse your sins.
- Come to me and I will bear your sicknesses,
- Come to me and I will be your strength in weakness,
- Come to me and I will comfort your sorrows,
- Come to me and I will deliver you from your demons,
- Come to me and I will give you rest.
- Come to me. Believe in me. Rest in me. Rest on me.

All things are possible—all the blessings, all the promises, all the provisions, and the goodnesses, and abundances, and surprises, and perfections, and transformations, and providences, and joys, and healings, and miracles, and protections, and love, and gifts, and mercies, and liberties, and hopes—all the things of grace are possible to the one who believes.

I'm writing all this, hoping to grow your faith, because hearing of grace in the Scriptures—which is what we're doing right now—is how faith grows.

5. FAITH GROWS - A Champion of Grace and Truth increases faith by hearing the Word of Christ, the Gospel of Grace, and the promises of God again and again. (Romans 10:17)

A grace based, Christ-filled sermon is a protein smoothie with extra dark chocolate and no gross vegetables in it—and it will put muscle on your faith so that all things are possible to the one who believes.

> "Immediately the father of the child cried out and said with tears, 'Lord, I believe; help my unbelief!'" (Mark 9:24)

His faith is so small that the man is worried it is too small. So he says, *Help my unbelief.* He's so worried for his son, that he can't stand the thought that his own unbelief would get in the way of his deliverance.

This is one of the doctrines of demons, by the way. Oh, says the demon, your faith is not enough. Too bad.

I'm writing to teach you that *if you have faith enough to ask God, you have faith enough.* If you have faith enough to pray you have faith enough.

This man is in hand-to-hand combat with a demon. He has been told that faith is the victory, so he declares it: "Lord I believe." He raises the Shield of Faith, however shaky his hands may be.

Then, however, he immediately fears because the devil whispers that his faith is too small. So he pleads, "Oh, please, help me in my unbelief."

I have good news for you: *weak faith is still faith.* Even a shaky hand can touch a solid rock. When we say that you are to become a champion of grace and truth, we do not mean that you will never shake, never falter, never doubt, or never fear.

We say that in the great conflict of spiritual warfare, you will press through your own doubts and fears, because there is a great secret the devil doesn't want you to know.

6. ASK - A Champion of Grace and Truth can still ask great things from God even with the smallest and shakiest faith.

You don't have to have it all together. You don't have to conquer all of your enemies. You just have to look to Jesus and believe, because faith is not the power, He is. The Shield of Faith is strong in Him, not in you.

And look at what happens.

> "When Jesus saw that the people came running together, He rebuked the unclean spirit, saying to it, 'Deaf and dumb spirit, I command you, come out of him and enter him no more!' Then the spirit cried out, convulsed him greatly, and came out of him. And he became as one dead, so that many said, 'He is dead.' But Jesus took him by the hand and lifted him up, and he arose." (Mark 9:25-27)

The dad comes with three gallons of unbelief and one teaspoon of faith, and that's enough.

Jesus proceeds to do the work which answered both his prayers, which are to help his unbelief, yes, but even more, to deliver his precious son.

This is such a powerful testimony of the way God brings you into your victory.

7. VICTORY - A Champion of Grace and Truth isn't scolded into victory, you're blessed into victory.

Christians don't enter victory by being scolded and lectured and beat up and shamed. That only produces guilt and that only produces hypocrisy.

You are blessed into victory. You are "gospelled" into victory — good news again and again.

More than anything else, the preacher's job, and the church's job is to open your eyes to the blessings God has already given you in Christ, so that you will claim your victory, so that you can kick the devil in the teeth and enjoy your blood-bought blessings as a believer in Jesus.

Amen.

THE CHRISTIAN IN COMPLETE ARMOR 211

We are talking about a believer who wears the Armor of God and who activates that armor with prayer.

We are saying that in this great battle against the demonic hosts of wickedness, against the strongholds of darkness, against the demons and even the devil himself, that you can be a champion of grace and truth in a demon-infested culture of confusion and pain.

And this is exactly what Jesus is going to say:

> "And when He had come into the house, His disciples asked Him privately, "Why could we not cast it out?" So He said to them, "This kind can come out by nothing but prayer ~~and fasting~~."" (Mark 9:28-29)

I don't want to shock anybody, but the words "and fasting" don't belong here. They are not in this verse in the original Greek.

Those words are a late addition, historically speaking. These words are omitted in the best ancient Greek manuscripts. My hunch is they were added by a legalistic scribe, trying to edit the Holy Spirit, and tying to explain the disciples' failure. These words are not in the NASB, NIV, ESV, NLT, or any modern, trustworthy translation. Plus, Jesus has already declared that while he is still with them, the disciples cannot fast (Mark 2:19). [Plus, a technical note for scholars: the USB4 has the omission at confidence level A, maximum confidence.]

So let's look at just what Jesus said. *This kind of demon can come out by nothing but prayer.*

When God put prayer into the hands of his people, he put a nuclear powerhouse on our lips.

But wait a minute.

Jesus says these words to answer the disciples' question about their failure. Why couldn't they evict the demon?

Are you telling me that a hurting man brings a demon-possessed boy to the disciples of Jesus, and they do everything they can think of, *but nobody thinks to pray?* Really? Is that even possible?

Yes, I think it's possible. I think we make the same mistake they made, and we do it all the time.

If you ever wonder why so many of your prayers bounce off the ceiling, maybe you're making the same mistake the disciples did.

It's the secret tucked away in verse 19. It's what the disciples failed to do until Jesus told them to do it. Jesus said: *"'Bring him to me.' Then they brought him to Him." (Mark 9:19, 20).*

The disciples did everything in prayer but bring this boy to Jesus.

I'm not saying they had to do that physically; I'm saying they had to bring him to Jesus in prayer. Bring him to the same one who just a few hours before was blazing in glory and shining in light and proving once for all that he his greater than the devil and the demons and all the evil they can ever spit into the world.

Jesus said, "Bring him to *me.*"

You know you can pray for a person without bringing that person to Jesus. That's a mistake.

You can pray for a need without bringing the need to Jesus.

You can pray for a thing and forget the power of the One who created that thing.

8. JESUS - The Champion of Grace and Truth prays every adversity and opportunity into the hands of Jesus, seated on his throne of grace and glory.

I don't care if you pray eloquent prayers or stammering prayers.

The power is not in the prayer. The power is the one to whom we pray.

Bring him to Jesus.

Bring her to Jesus.

Bring yourself to Jesus.

Hand everything over. Let it go.

No demon, no addiction, no depression, no trouble, no anger, no sadness, no failure, no sin, no dysfunction, no poverty, no devil can triumph when Jesus is near.

Let's wear our armor, and let's be those champions of Grace and Truth in a culture of pain and confusion.

I promise you won't be bored.

REFLECTION AND DISCUSSION

1. How much do you want to be a Spiritual Champion?
2. In the battle between good and evil, Satan and God, angels and demons are you more a part of the problem or the solution? Why?
3. What are 3 or 4 ways your life will be different as a result of reading this book?
4. Why do you think the disciples did *everything but* bring the boy to Jesus? Why is it that Jesus implies they didn't pray?
5. How does Ephesians 6:19-20 connect our armor with our mission of helping lost people get saved?

CHAPTER 16
ONE THOUGHT TO RULE THEM ALL

When thoughts or inclinations contrary to the will and ways of God creep in, many dear Christians mistake these miserable orphans for their own children, and take upon themselves the full responsibility for these carnal passions. So deftly does the devil slip his own thoughts into the saints' bosom that by the time they begin to whimper, he is already out of sight. And the Christian, seeing no one but himself at home, supposes these misbegotten notions are his own. So he bears the shame himself, and Satan has accomplished his purpose.
~William Gurnall

SOMETHING DEEP

"For though we walk in the flesh, we do not war according to the flesh. For the weapons of our warfare are not carnal but mighty in God for pulling down strongholds, casting down arguments and every high thing that exalts itself against the knowledge of God,

bringing every thought into captivity to the obedience of Christ."
(2 Corinthians 10:3-5)

In this verse, Paul lifts the veil and lets us see what's going on in the background—the spiritual realities behind all history, and behind the story of our lives. We live every day of our lives in the crossfire of the invisible cosmic conflict between Satan and God. This is spiritual warfare on an epic scale.

Even more, Paul declares this warfare to be *our* warfare. Nobody sits this one out.

Can you imagine what you would see right now if God lifted the veil and let you peek into the spiritual realm, wherever you are reading this book? Can you imagine actually seeing angels and demons battle, seeing the glory of God shining down, right there, wherever you are?

Throughout this book I have suggested that this cosmic conflict plays out in every conflict of our lives. Emotional. Spiritual. Psychological. Physical.

Where there is human brokenness, the devil is not far away.

Where there is pain, addiction, drunkenness, adultery, pornography, idols, suicidal ideation, hatred, bitterness, and cruelty—all of these things go deeper than human origin. They are spiritual at the core.

So, you are called as a Christian soldier. You are called to demolish strongholds. You are called to "take every thought captive to the obedience of Christ."

In 2 Corinthians 10:3-5, Paul unveils a huge open secret about living your life in the victory that Christ has already won in his Cross and resurrection.

If you want to be whole, happy, and blessed. If you want to live out the abundant life Jesus promised you. If you want to have a bigger impact in your life for Christ and the gospel. And if you want to really brandish the holy weapons of your warfare, then you need the open secret revealed in this verse.

ONE THOUGHT TO RULE THEM ALL

I'd like to go back to that phrase, "the obedience of Christ." Paul writes the words, "taking every thought captive to the obedience of Christ."

It's an interesting phrase and a little bit tricky. That word "obedience" indicates submission and respect. Of course, that should be true of our lives.

But before we can talk about our obedience *to* Christ, I want to talk about the obedience *of* Christ.

1. OBEDIENCE: Jesus came into this world as Lord of All, but he submitted himself to the Father's plan that he might save his people from their sins.

How does that work?

Jesus was two natures in one person. He was truly God, that's his divine nature. He was truly human, that's his human nature.

Some things in the life of Jesus flow from his human nature. Some things flow from his divine nature. Some things flow from the union of the two natures in one person.

The Bible teaches us that Jesus actually obeyed God the Father: "And being found in appearance as a man, He humbled Himself and became obedient to the point of death, even the death of the cross" (Philippians 2:8).

Jesus submitted to the Father. He condescended. He humbled himself. Specifically, he became obedient to the point of death, even the death of the Cross.

That is what saves us. That is what gives us eternal life. That is what makes us Christians, when we believe. That is also what establishes is in victory in this great cosmic conflict of the ages.

All of the obedience, all of the submission—everything that happened that day that the Son of God laid down his celestial crown, set aside his shimmering robes, and stepped down to this cold, cruel world—all of his obedience to the plan of God was laser-beam focused on one place, one time, one event: He became obedient to the point of death.

The "obedience *of* Christ" is another way of talking about that moment of death, his saving work on the Cross. This is important.

We can see the same thing in another place, when Paul writes, "For as by one man's disobedience many were made sinners, so also by one Man's obedience many will be made righteous" (Romans 5:19).

"By one man's disobedience, many were made sinners..." Who is that one man? Adam. What was his disobedience? Eating the forbidden fruit.

Then flip it over.

"So also by one Man's obedience..." Who is that one man? Jesus Christ. What specifically was his "obedience" that makes us righteous? His sacrificial death on Calvary's cross.

He became sin for us that we might be made the righteousness of God in Him (2 Corinthians 5:21).

The way the Bible authors write, they use the phrase, "the obedience of Christ" to point to the abject humiliation of his death on the Cross.

When the Bible talks about the obedience of Christ, that's the focus. Calvary. Grace. Salvation.

We have this same connection again from the Author of Hebrews, speaking of Jesus, who "though He was a Son, yet He learned obedience by the things which He suffered" (Hebrews 5:8).

Again, Scripture links the "obedience of Christ" to the sufferings of Christ on the cross for our salvation.

You have a Savior. His name is Jesus. There is a specific action that Jesus did to be your Savior. That specific action is that he shed his precious blood and died on the cross. This death was horrific. Punishing. Painful. It was the epitome of human suffering. It was a humiliation unlike any other. The Son of God laid aside the pleasure of heaven, was stripped naked, beaten to a bloody pulp, spit upon, blindfolded, punched in the face, skinned alive with a whip (scourged), crowned with thorns, hit in the head with a club, nailed to a cross, and lifted up to die.

Even worse than all that—if such a thing is even imaginable—the awful crimes, the heinous sins, and the arrogant iniquities of every human's life were poured out on him. So awful was this moment that God shrouded it in darkness. That is when Jesus cried out. That is when he began "roaring" (Psalm 22:1, KJV). He cried out in such unfathomable pain because he was forsaken of God. God was judging him, punishing him, and damning him for all our sins. There is no moment so dreadful, no suffering so horrible, no mystery so dark, and no humiliation so complete as this substitutionary death of our Lord upon Calvary's Cross.

Why did he endure all this? Why did he die? He died because he loves you and this was the only way to pay the penalty for your sins, to satisfy the demands of divine justice, so that a holy God could love you without compromising his character, so that you could be reconciled to God.

He died so he could crush Satan's head and win a mighty victory on your behalf.

He was thinking of you when he was nailed to the Cross.

He knew you by name, and he had you in mind, when he absorbed your sins. Has there ever been a love like this?

This is what Scripture means by speaking of the "obedience of Christ."

The heart of everything that matters is the obedience of Christ to the point of his death on the cross. We cherish the old rugged Cross. We preach the old rugged Cross. We cling to the old rugged Cross.

That old Cross makes our hearts tender. That old Cross, when we hear of it and really think of it, brings a tear to our eye. The Cross of Christ is everything.

Here is the point of this discussion:

All of the glory, all of the suffering, all of the history, all of the meaning, all of the blessing, all of the horror, all of the pain, all of the theology, all of the doctrine, all of the love, all of the graciousness, and all the gifts of that one, stupendous, never-to-be-repeated act is summed up in one transcendent and paradoxical phrase: *the obedience of Christ.*

2. THE CROSS: The Obedience of Christ is another way of focusing on the Finished Work of Christ on the Cross.

Now, let's bring this back to spiritual warfare. I want to bring in two episodes from the life of Jesus, and then bring it all together. We have already seen that embarrassing moment when Jesus called Peter Satan.

> "But He turned and said to Peter, 'Get behind Me, Satan! You are an offense to Me, for you are not mindful of the things of God, but the things of men.'" (Matthew 16:23)

Two verses prior to this, Matthew tells us: "From that time Jesus began to show to His disciples that He must go to Jerusalem, and suffer many things from the elders and chief priests and scribes, and be killed, and be raised the third day." (Matthew 16:21)

Jesus is teaching his disciples the heart and soul of his whole ministry: that he will suffer and die and then be raised again. Calvary is the main thing.

Jesus teaches on Calvary, and it is at this point that Peter objects. "Then Peter took Him aside and began to rebuke Him, saying, 'Far be it from You, Lord; this shall not happen to You!'" (Matthew 16:22)

And that's when Jesus whirls around and calls Peter Satan.

Why? Jesus explains why. "Because you have in your mind not the things of God, but the things of men."

Your mind has thoughts in it, Peter, that come from Satan. They are not reality, they are unreality. They are not truth, they are lies. Those thoughts go exactly opposite of the gospel, Peter.

Jesus is saying that when you look at God's plan from a human perspective, instead of from God's perspective, you are displaying a profound problem. *That profound problem is that a satanic philosophy has taken root in your mind.*

The proof that a satanic philosophy has taken root in your mind is that you actually speak out *against* the Cross of Christ, and against the sufficiency of Christ's death. "Far be it from you, Lord, this shall not happen to you."

This is what happened in Peter's mind, but Jesus saw Satan lurking in the shadows.

So he turns on Peter and calls him out for letting the devil stick that thought into his head.

Judas did the same thing: "And supper being ended, the devil having already put it into the heart of Judas Iscariot, Simon's son, to betray Him..." (John 13:2)

It was in that same scene that Jesus knelt down and washed his disciples' feet—an emblem his coming humiliation.

I don't know how this works and I'm not sure of all that this means, but according to this verse, the devil was able to put something into the heart of Judas, which was to betray Jesus.

It is fair to conclude that Satan can put thoughts into your mind, thoughts into your heart.

I don't think the devil can *read* our minds. The Bible says that *only* God knows the human heart (1 Kings 8:39). However, the devil *has* had thousand of years of surveillance of the human race. He watches. He observes. He sees. His hosts of demons take notes. They can read us like a book, even if they can't know our thoughts. Satan knows your "tells."

So no, I don't think Satan can read our minds. But I do see in Scripture that he can put thoughts into our minds.

He did it here with Judas. It says so. "The devil put it into his heart to betray Jesus."

He did it with Peter, and put it into his heart to try to talk Jesus down from the Cross.

Later on, he did it with two horrible people named Ananias and Sapphira" "But Peter said, 'Ananias, why has Satan filled your heart to lie to the Holy Spirit...'" (Acts 5:3). Centuries earlier, Satan put evil thoughts into King David's mind (1 Chronicles 21:1).

So the devil can't read our minds, but he can put thoughts into our minds. Therefore, let's say:

3. COLONIZE: Satan's endgame is to colonize our minds through high-sounding nonsense masquerading as philosophy or religion.

Satan is a teacher. Satan is a philosopher. Satan is a culture warrior. Satan is a community organizer. He is a social media influencer, a news anchor, and a preacher.

They used to call this brainwashing. Today, I think the word would be grooming. Or indoctrination.

Satan's diabolical passion is to *normalize unreality.*

Unreality is simply another word for evil. Some call it *crazy*. Some call it *outrageous*. Some call it *insane*. To be correct, it should be called *evil*; never forget it.

His Infernal Majesty has a gradual way of infiltrating the deepest parts of your thinking with ideas and opinions and moral values that crawled out of the sewers of hell, and were wrapped in popular, nice-sounding packaging.

The devil's strategy is to colonize your mind with high sounding nonsense.

I don't think the devil does this directly. Most of the time, it's indirect.

Most of the time, the lies come into our minds through the gates of culture, art, media, social media, music, government, academia, entertainment, online, digital, and on and on.

The whole world-system is the devil's misinformation campaign.

When a culture turns away from God, it believes demonic lies. These demonic lies become institutionalized. The whole cultural system of values and beliefs gets demonized. Literally demonized. This is a condition the Bible calls "strong delusion" (2 Thessalonians 2:11). It is the inevitable consequence of continually disrespecting God.

Have you ever considered that there may be whole structures of thoughts in your mind that have been constructed by the dark side, and are in sync with the devil?

How would you know?

First, by the Word, and second, by their fruit: Addiction, depression, hostility, broken relationships, unresolved anger, bitterness, sexual addiction, sexual perversion, religion, legalism, self-righteousness, a fractured heart, and, finally, a heart that is not tender toward Jesus Christ.

God loves you, and you have some rehab to do.

By the way, these are called strongholds, and in this book we have talked about strongholds extensively.

All of this brings us back right where we started, and to the one thought to rule them all.

THE ONE THOUGHT

> "For the weapons of our warfare are not carnal but mighty in God for pulling down strongholds, casting down arguments and every high thing that exalts itself against the knowledge of God, bringing every thought into captivity to the obedience of Christ." (2 Corinthians 10:4-5)

All those thoughts, all of that stream of internal dialogue, all of those uncontrollable drives and persistent ideation is to be brought "into captivity to the obedience of Christ."

It may seem odd, but this is the biggest truth I want to leave you with after fifteen chapters on spiritual warfare.

But what does it mean to bring a thought "captive" to "the obedience of Christ"?

It's a tricky little phrase. Different Bible translations go in different directions.

- NIV: we take captive every thought to make it obedient to Christ.
- NLT: We capture their rebellious thoughts and teach them to obey Christ.
- ESV: and take every thought captive to obey Christ.
- NKJV: bringing every thought into captivity to the obedience of Christ.
- NASB: and we are taking every thought captive to the obedience of Christ.

The question is on that little phrase "the obedience of Christ." What exactly does it mean? What exactly is the relationship between obedience and Christ? Precisely whose obedience is in view?

The grammatical structure here is, one again, called a genitive. We have two nouns (obedience, Christ) joined by the word "of." What does it mean? With this genitive, we can go in two directions, and both options are grammatically legit. Earlier, we identified a couple of genitive structures. Here, we have two more.

Stick with me; I promise fireworks.

1. Option One: bring every thought captive to make it obedient to Christ. (This is called the objective genitive.)

2. Option Two: bring every thought captive to Christ's obedience to the plan of God. (This is called the subjective genitive.)

I spent hours working on this one phrase, this one bit of Greek grammar. I can tell you that the Bible commentaries are unanimous in choosing Option one.

Under this interpretation, *we are to bring every thought captive so that your thoughts, and therefore your life-choices, are obedient to Christ.*

There is truth in that, and, for the record, I am pro-obedience. I'm all for it. Our lives should be obedient to Christ.

But I hereby respectfully and humbly disagree with the bulk of Bible commentaries. Whenever I do that and go out on a limb mostly by myself, I feel an obligation to explain why. I don't want anybody to think they should believe me without evidence, or just because I say so.

So, let me make my case.

First, I have yet to find a commentary that even bothers to make the case for option one, or even considers option two. All of the dozens of commentaries that I have checked just *assume* Option One. This is something that I call "the commentary echo chamber" but I won't get into that.

The librarian at Simpson University (Redding CA), after several hours, finally helped me get hold of a scholarly journal article from 2011 by a Bible professor from Wheaton College. Michael Kibbe writes:

"In grammatical terms, I will argue that τοῦ Χριστοῦ [of Christ] should be read as a subjective rather than an objective genitive. I prefer to say "Christ's obedience… This essay will suggest that the phrase τὴν ὑπακοὴν τοῦ Χριστοῦ [the obedience of Christ] in 2 Corinthians 10:5 refers to "Christ's obedience" rather than "obedience to Christ."[1]

Listen, this book isn't a seminary textbook, I get that. So no details. I just feel an obligation that if I'm going to go out on a limb all alone, I owe it to you to at least tell you there's a strong case for this interpretation. I am convinced that the strongest case can be made against the common interpretation, and for the one I'm giving you today.

Which is this:

When the Bible tells you to tear down the demonic strongholds, and to clean out all the toxic crud that has infiltrated your mind, and when the Bible tells you to bring every thought into captivity to the obedience of Christ... *it is not talking about you obeying Christ, it's talking about Christ obeying the divine plan of eternal salvation, and you fixing your mind on HIM doing THAT.*

Let that sink in. Read it as many times as you need to. You are not bringing your thoughts into captivity so *you* can obey Christ because your obedience is not the point of this verse. *It's Christ's obedience to death on the Cross.*

What does this mean?

4. GOSPEL: The power of the Gospel is the divine kryptonite to vaporize the dysfunctional strongholds the devil has snaked into your heart.

Touch the devil's lies with Gospel truth, and they vaporize.

Bring every thought into alignment with his sacrifice.

Bring every though into adjustment with the finished work of Christ.

When your thoughts of guilt touch Calvary Love, they vaporize.

When voices of condemnation run into Romans 8:1, they are muzzled.

When your doubts and fears meet "the Lord is my shepherd I shall not lack..." they lose their power. (Psalm 23:1).

When devil and nearby demons see you running through

Ephesians 6 and putting on your armor, he will flee from you (James 4:7).

When your temptations come under the sound of Calvary's Love, they lose the power because "Sin shall not have dominion over you for you are not under law but under grace." (Romans 6:14)

CAPTIVATED

5. ONE THOUGHT: The one thought to rule them all is the Finished Work of Christ, along with the rich tapestry of interconnected, transcendent truths that the Cross entails.

Keep growing in grace. Keep going deeper in the Word of Christ. Keep your heart in the love of God.

Bring all your thoughts to the foot of the Cross, and lay them there. Some will be affirmed. Some will melt. Some will explode.

Whatever thoughts are left standing will make you a champion of grace and truth in a culture of confusion and pain.

Tell your thoughts of guilt and shame and tell your self-punishing drives: "There is therefore now no condemnation for those who are in Christ Jesus."

Tell all your fears that the Savior who shed blood for you will never leave you or forsake you.

Tell your Inner Victim that God has declared you more than a conqueror.

Tell your voices of addiction and "stuckness" you've been redeemed by the blood, and you are *free*.

You're bringing every thought captive to the obedience of Christ.

Tell that script in your head that says, "I'll never change," that your God makes all things new. That thought that says you're doomed, that voice that says you'll never be happy, that whisper that tells you life's not worth living tell them all you have a Savior who shed his blood for your abundant life, and you claim that life by faith.

And that thought that keeps telling you God has let you down, take that thought by the hand, and show that thought,

Jesus Christ, bleeding on that Cross. Then look together at that empty grave. Then take that thought and look up into the heavenly realm, and see Jesus, enthroned there, representing you, and making intercession for you. See him building a mansion for you, and being your mediator, your protector, and your ever-present help. Show that thought how Jesus is your friend, guardian, guide, provider, victory, sufficiency, sacrifice, Savior, Supporter, and your soon and coming King. After all this, ask that voice to tell you again how God has let you down.

Victory is the day when every thought is held captive by Calvary Love, captivated by the love of God made possible by the obedience of Christ.

> VICTORY IS THE DAY WHEN EVERY THOUGHT IS HELD CAPTIVE BY CALVARY LOVE.

That is the weapon of our warfare.
That is the armor that is mighty in God.
That is psychological wholeness.
That is the end of addiction.
That is the depth of forgiveness.
That is demonic deliverance.
That is the power of love.
That is the glory of Grace.
That is the fight of faith.
That is the believer's authority.
We need you. The world needs you. The Church needs you. Our

children need you. Let's go. Let's push back the darkness. Let's crush the devil's lies. Let's walk in victory.

Put on the Armor of God, today, tomorrow, and every day. Push back the darkness. Reject the hive-mind of Borg-like compliance to heartbreaking lies and doctrines of demons. Stand strong, stand all, and stand proud in the victory of Jesus, our Savior forever. Step daily into the sunny highlands of the Promised Land, our glorious birthright by the matchless grace of God.

Make a difference for Christ and the Gospel. You can do it. God will be your strength.

I am excited to see the levels of victory you experience as you become The Christian in Complete Armor.

REFLECTION AND DISCUSSION

Instead of questions, I'd like to leave you with this classic hymn on Spiritual Warfare for your edification. Pray and think through these powerful lyrics.

> *Soldiers of Christ, arise, and put your armor on,*
> *Strong in the strength which God supplies thro' His eternal Son;*
> *Strong in the Lord of Hosts and in His mighty pow'r,*
> *Who in the strength of Jesus trusts is more than conqueror.*
>
> *Stand then in His great might, with all His strength endued,*
> *And take, to aid you for the fight, the panoply of God.*
> *From strength to strength go on, wrestle and fight and pray;*
> *Tread all the pow'rs of darkness down and win the well-fought day.*

Leave no unguarded place, no weakness of the soul;
Take every virtue, every grace, and fortify the whole.
That, having all things done and all your conflicts past,
Ye may o'ercome thro' Christ alone and stand entire at last.

CHARLES WESLEY, 1749

---

1. Michael Kibbe. "The Obedience of Christ": A Reassessment of τὴν ὑπακοὴν τοῦ Χριστοῦ in 2 Corinthians 10:5. Journal for the Study of Paul and His Letters 2(1):41-56. 2012-04-01. 21592063

EPILOGUE

Almighty God, today, I put on the full armor of God.
I put on the *Belt of Truth*, to understand the times in which I live.
I put on the *Breastplate of Righteousness*, to guard and protect my heart.
I put on the *Boots of the Gospel*, for my solid footing and my mission in a hurting world.
I take up the *Shield of Faith*, to believe my God no matter what.
I wear the *Helmet of Salvation*, to guard my mind from delusion and despair.
I carry the *Sword of the Spirit*, to defeat the darkness and lift high the Cross.
I declare myself a soldier of the Cross.
I stand in the Victory of Christ.
I make you, God, my stronghold today.
Amen.

ALSO BY BILL GIOVANNETTI

Deepen Your Walk With God and Expand Your Influence for the Gospel

If you'd like to go deeper in God's Word, Bill Giovannetti has launched an online Bible school with seminary-level teaching for lay people. Find out more at VeritasSchool.life. Deepen your walk with God and widen your impact for the Gospel. You can get started today at no cost.

Selected Books

The Grace Pathway: Ten Books on Spiritual Growth and Discipleship

Mindgames: Rising Above Other People's Craziness (A Lifestyle Commentary on Esther)

Chaos: As Goes the Church So Goes the World

Grace Intervention

Grace Rehab

Grace Breakthrough

Available on Amazon or wherever books are sold.
https://amzn.to/47sbwem

www.ingramcontent.com/pod-product-compliance
Lightning Source LLC
Chambersburg PA
CBHW072001110526
44592CB00012B/1168